fusions

fusions

MARTIN WEBB
RICHARD WHITTINGTON

a new look at Australian cooking

SOMA
san francisco

First published 1997 by Ebury Press, Random House UK, and Random House Australia. North American
Edition published 1998 by SOMA Books, by arrangement with Ebury Press.

SOMA Books is an imprint of Bay Books & Tapes, Inc. For information, please contact Bay books & Tapes, 555
De Haro St., No. 220, San Francisco, CA 94107.

for the SOMA edition:
Publisher: James Connolly
Art Director: Jeffrey O'Rourke
Production: Patrick Barber Design
Proofreader: Marianna Cherry

for the original Ebury Press edition:
Editor: Lews Esson
Design: Vanessa Courtier
Photography: Earl Carter
Styling: Wanda Tucker
Food for Photography: Martin Webb

Library of Congress Cataloging-in-Publication Data
Webb, Martin.
   Fusions: a new look at Australian cooking / Martin Webb, Richard Whittington.
      p. cm.
   Originally published: London : Ebury Press ; Australia : Random House, 1997.
   Includes index.
   ISBN 1-57959-013-6
   1. Cookery, Australian. I. Whittington, Richard. II. Title.
   TX725.A8W43 1998
   641.5994--DC21   98-10621
                                                             CIP

Color reproduction by Colourpath
Printed and bound in Singapore by Tien Wah Press

10 9 8 7 6 5 4 3 2 1

Distributed to the trade by Publishers Group West

contents

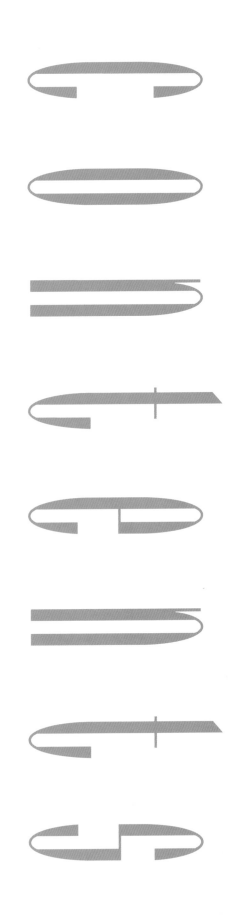

introduction

Australia today is an exhilarating place for anybody interested in cooking, a new world with new perceptions and all the appropriate skills to develop and fuse the best aspects of the diverse food cultures that make up the global kitchen. While seeking to push the boundaries out, the central message remains simplicity and the resulting food is light, vibrant with flavor and absolutely of the millennium — food that looks as good as it tastes. The only thing that governs the creative cooking process here is whether or not a dish works.

Contemporary Australian cooking, with its emphasis on quality of ingredients and balance, is an essentially healthy diet driven by changing perceptions of how imaginatively a menu can be written. In this we can find many parallels with Californian cooking, for both have taken inspiration from a melting pot of different cultures and with Southeast Asia as strong an influence there as it undoubtedly is in Australia. Neither place has the constriction of a single culinary heritage — though California does have a strong Mexican/Spanish history — and both have enthusiastically embraced a heady *mélange* of tastes and textures. Australian cooks have the confidence to recognize in California a kindred spirit when it might be easier to pretend that no synergy exists and that there are no lessons to be learned from a place which,

in all honesty, paved the way for a style that is identifiably of the Pacific Rim.

Notably in Australia a similar development has been achieved without loss of national identity, a quality that shines through the veneer of multiculturalism, expressing a character of great pride and unity of purpose, and resulting in food defined by beautifully fresh local produce as much as by the vast continent itself, indigenous ingredients and vastly different microclimates. The cities have wonderful markets that happily combine wholesale and retail in the same locations. Sydney's fish market, for example, is breathtaking in its scale, with as many as 200 species on offer, while Queen Victoria market in Melbourne offers everything from skillfully prepared meat to Southeast Asian fruits, vegetables and spices.

In the country, cheesemakers and specialist farmers abound, their burgeoning artisanal production flagging a food culture in the ascendant. Farmers are becoming more and more specialized, developing niche markets, such as miniature vegetables for restaurants, or seeing opportunities to create new lines of supply internationally. The farming of yabbies — freshwater crayfish — in sheep waterholes in Western Australia is a case in point, while in southern New South Wales Illabo milk-fed lamb is highly prized. Queensland, once known principally for its sugarcane and Bunderberg rum, today supplies the nation with tropical fruits, including mangoes, mangosteens, rambutans, lychees and papayas, all now exported to a world hungry for new flavors and textures. More familiar berries grow in abundance, including blackberries, raspberries, boysenberries, blueberries and cape gooseberries. The latest agricultural techniques are applied, with hydroponics being used to grow all kinds of green vegetables all year round. Queensland is also a major source of kangaroo meat for expanding domestic and export markets, and the wild pig sold in German butcher shops may well have been shot here.

The sea offers whiting and fine game fish like yellow fin tuna and Spanish mackerel, while closer to shore the reefs teem with snapper, red emperor, parrot fish, coral trout and wrasse. Mangrove swamps are the home for giant mud crab, which can weigh four pounds and upward, while smaller blue swimmer crabs are to be found just off the sandy beaches. Moreton Bay Bugs, alarmingly alien-looking crustacea with delicious sweet meaty tails, are another regional delicacy, while prawns (shrimp) of every size and type abound: school prawns, Bay prawns, banana prawns, so called because of their size, and farmed black tiger prawns. King Island,

situated between the Australian South West coast and Tasmania, has become an extraordinary center of dairy excellence, while Tasmania itself has pioneered organic salmon farming and quality smoking of the results. Everywhere you look in Australia you see enthusiasm and dedication, resulting in the kind of achievement that only comes from personal commitment. There is a strong sense of progress, of new ideas being transformed rapidly into professional practice.

In a kitchen rooted in diversity, the dangers of being a magpie cook are all too apparent. If you never sit still and think about what you are doing and why you are doing it, or if you never work within one idiom for any length of time, things can become shallow and merely imitative, the delivery lacking substance. In an increasingly international culinary context, where information is globally and rapidly disseminated, bright young chefs and keen private cooks can absorb new ideas each week wherever they live and work, spinning through a big wheel of possibilities before moving on to the next fashionable idea. There is plenty of conscious fashion and style in Australia's restaurants and private dining rooms but, for all the country's youthfulness as a center of culinary excellence, its chefs are generally more mature than their counterparts elsewhere in the confident treatment of the dazzling color palette of tastes and textures that living on the Pacific Rim affords. Australian cooks seem to get the sensitive "mixing and matching" side of things right more often than they get it wrong, recognizing that eclectic dishes are not always a good idea, that there has to be understanding and a sense of balance before disparate ingredients can be made to combine harmoniously.

Frequently, the description "eclectic" when applied to food has become pejorative, synonymous with awkwardness and pretension, when its true meaning is the very opposite, simply suggesting a lack of constraint, an openness and willingness to experiment and, when it does not work, to put it in the trash and try something else. The ability to embrace Southeast Asian flavors without allowing them to dominate a menu is an essential part of the new Australian food vocabulary, which also encompasses French, Italian and Greek influences and which is brave enough to look toward North Africa and the Middle East with the same acquisitive gaze.

Australia, however, is not a place that eschews the past nor one that insists that everything be mixed and matched. Excellent national restaurants are very much a part of the bigger picture, whether you want to eat French, Italian or Japanese food at its

best and without a stalk of lemongrass or a peanut in sight. Fine beef and lamb will always benefit from the simplest treatments and nowhere has better quality meat than Australia. The barbecue is still the icon of domestic entertaining, as much a lifestyle statement as the Thai restaurant around every corner, though today it is just as likely to provide the heat to cook green-lipped mussels under a cover as it is to grill a steak.

In attempting to define Australian cooking today, one begins with the most obvious phenomenon, that much of it is fusion food at its best, that is, imaginative dishes created in an environment where the whole world provides inspiration but where people choose local produce to shape their long-term direction. The nuances and subtleties, the finer shades that position and differentiate that elusive Australian quality, come from the aromatic counterpoints borrowed from China, Thailand, Indonesia, Malaysia, Vietnam, India, Singapore and Japan but, equally important, from the Mediterranean. The most recent element to be taken on board is, ironically, that of native Australian produce, the "bush tucker" of Aboriginal diet, with its unique fruits, seeds and nuts, including eucalyptus, wattle seed and pepperleaf, and the alternative meat sources of kangaroo, emu, buffalo and crocodile.

It is an exuberant rollercoaster of a cuisine, that triumphantly celebrates more highs than lows, a place where once you understand the rules, it is perfectly all right to break them. Techniques, too, intertwine and cross over. The wok is no longer the exclusive preserve of Asian kitchens. The ridged grill and charcoal grill are now ubiquitous, as is the bamboo steamer, no longer capable of association with one nation or one place. Traditional ways of doing things sit on top of different traditional approaches. They cross and merge and new food results.

Despite the obvious parallels with California, it has to be said that Australia's oldest culinary umbilicus is to England, perhaps not as dazzling a historical association as the American West's retrospective links with Mexico and Spain, but of lasting importance nonetheless. In common with the British, Australians remember the arrival of the first avocado in the sixties, a time when meat was served uniformly gray while vegetables were cooked to perdition. The food revolution started in both countries as much in the home as in restaurants. Wine and food societies played a significant part in raising awareness in both countries, with Sydney's Society of Gourmets being particularly influential in its championing of food and wine as meaningful partners. Serious cooking schools in both countries first opened at the end of

the sixties, a commercial consequence of a changing perception that the domestic kitchen was a place for pleasure as much as functionality or drudgery. The sixties also saw in Australia the phenomenon of Bring-Your-Owns, small unlicensed restaurants that mimicked the French bistro and offered affordable food in simple surroundings. BYO is now a way of life, with even the grandest licensed restaurants happy for customers to drink the wines they bring with them, a recognition of how many knowledgeable wine enthusiasts there are.

Australia's Elizabeth David was and remains Joan Campbell, now in her eighties but as redoubtable, wickedly funny and talented as ever, still redefining good food as this is written. If anybody ever demonstrates the veracity of the French saying, you never grow old at the table, it is she. While excellent restaurants abound, notably and most prolifically in the nation's twin dining capitals of Sydney and Melbourne, the changes are driven increasingly in Australia through a developed culture of entertaining at home, which means eating outside for a lot of the year and, for many people, eating in the kitchen. This inextricably links a style of living with a style of eating, a phenomenon celebrated in the world's most influential food magazine, *Vogue Entertaining*, published every two months in Sydney but snapped up by discerning food lovers all over the world.

Style here does not necessarily imply crystal goblets and damask linen, but often a much more minimalist and simple framework, where the table is quite likely to be covered with heavy paper and the wines drunk from Duralex tumblers. The food may not be structured as first course, main course and dessert, nor would people expect it to be, since formality is thankfully low on the list of priorities. The quality of the ingredients comes first and the key is to entertain without snobbery or pretension. It is a very democratic pleasure principle, where inexpensive is not a dirty word.

In this context and as part of a lifestyle that can involve eating different dishes in different café-bistro locations, Australians have inevitably embraced a café society. Coffee drinking at all times of the day and night has become integral to social interaction, with knowledgeable consumers demanding and getting precisely the roast and style of coffee they want. Whole streets in Sydney, Melbourne and Perth are lined with cafés, bars, food shops and small restaurants.

Ten years ago, Australian chefs traveled to work in the best restaurants of Europe and the US, honing skills to take back home. Today their talent is being exported and, like Australian winemakers who have changed wine production and wine styles globally, their informed plurality will impact and influence the

way food is cooked and served the world over. Recently, Terence Conran, always shrewd in spotting trends before the competition, noted that while Australian chefs have great energy and wonderful raw materials to work on, more than anything their food ascendancy is about timing.

"Suddenly there is a moment when a generation of young people decides — this is what I want to do. In the Sixties it was pop music and hairdressing; in the Seventies fashion design or photography. In the Eighties everyone wanted to be a designer and, curiously, in the Nineties they want to be involved with food in one way or another. You have wonderful raw materials in Australia. You have young people who are reasonably affluent, you have a designer/media fraternity interested in the look of things. Together they are putting the flavor back into food. The rest of the world has much to learn from them."

This is a book that celebrates that heady moment of ascendancy, with recipes that epitomize the contemporary Australian cooking experience. This is food inspired by a time of change and expansion, fusions that bring us happily to the turn of a century. This is real food and honest food, but ultimately it is Australian food expressed through recipes that anybody can cook at home and with ingredients that are now universally available.

introduction

10

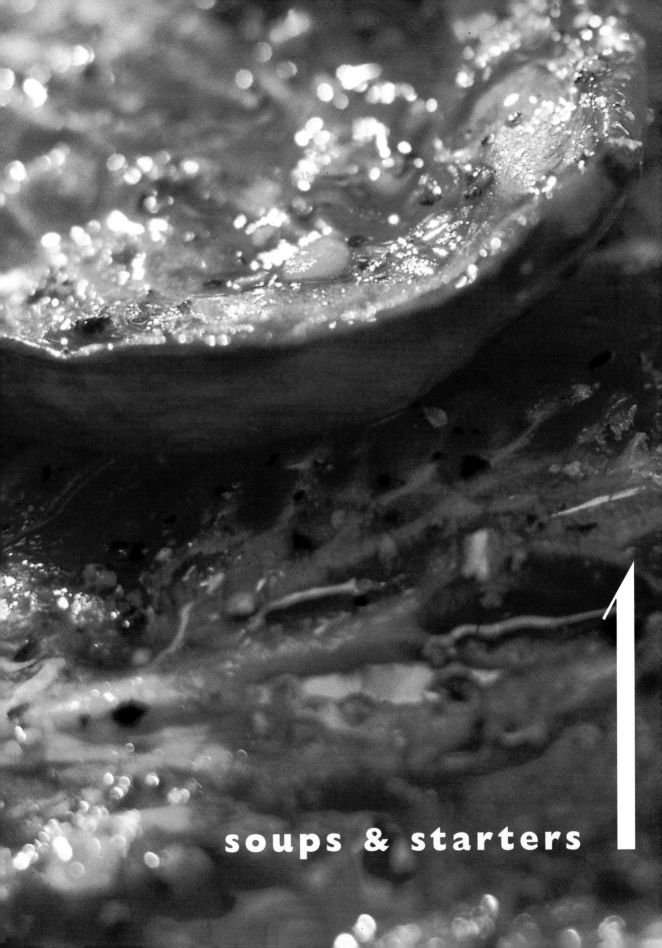

soups & starters

1

oxtail broth with star anise

One of the characteristics of Southeast Asian cooking is that meat is never browned before stewing. This has little or no effect on the flavor of the finished dish, but does give a very different appearance. The most forceful of all spices is star anise, which, used judiciously, imbues any slow-cooked dish with its delicate yet unmistakable fragrance. A heavy hand with this ingredient will, however, result in an overly powerful presence, dominating everything. Steamed jasmine rice goes well with this dish, as does a Chili Sambal (page 48).

2¼ pounds oxtails, cut into
  pieces
1 cinnamon stick
3 cloves
3 star anise
2 black cardamom pods
¼ teaspoon peppercorns
¼ teaspoon coriander seeds
1½-inch piece fresh ginger,
  peeled and sliced
3½ quarts light beef or chicken
  stock (page 152)
4 boiling onions
2 large carrots, cut into ½-inch
  rounds
½ cup sunflower oil
4 shallots, thinly sliced
1 cup fresh cilantro leaves

serves 4

Trim off as much fat as you can from the oxtail pieces. Put them in a large pan with the spices tied in a piece of cheesecloth and the ginger. Pour over the stock and bring to a boil, skimming. Turn down the heat and simmer gently for 2 to 3 hours, still skimming at regular intervals.

Add the onions (peeled but left whole) with the carrots and continue to simmer for a further 30 minutes.

Put the oil in a frying pan over medium heat. Fry the shallots, stirring, until golden brown. Transfer to paper towels to drain. By now the meat should be starting to fall off the bone.

Remove the oxtails from the pan, putting one or two pieces in each of 4 warmed deep bowls. Divide the carrots and onions equally among them and ladle the stock over. Scatter over whole cilantro leaves and finish with the crispy fried shallots.

asian-spiced stuffed cabbage in broth

You could argue that this is not so much a soup as a main course. Or you could serve it as a soup broth followed by the cabbage as a separate course. You need to use a Savoy-type cabbage; those round hard Dutch types are unsuitable. Indeed, as a general rule, white hard cabbages are not for cooking at all, other than as sauerkraut. Cantonese cured pork sausages (lop chong), available from most Chinese markets, are succulent and delicious when steamed.

8 ounces Chinese cured pork
  sausages
1 Savoy cabbage, 2¼ to 3 pounds
4 tablespoons sunflower oil
8 ounces onions, diced
2 garlic cloves, finely chopped
½ teaspoon cumin seeds
1 teaspoon peppercorns
2 teaspoons black mustard seeds
1 teaspoon red pepper flakes
1 pound ground pork
2 tablespoons fish sauce
2 cups fresh white bread crumbs
1 lemongrass stalk, hard outer
  leaves removed and thinly sliced
1 tablespoon chopped fresh flat-
  leaf parsley
1 egg
salt and pepper
2 quarts chicken stock (page
  152)
1 small bunch fresh chives

for 8 as soup,
4 as main course

Wash the sausage, steam it for 20 minutes and reserve. Cut out the base of the cabbage and blanch in rapidly boiling salted water for 5 to 8 minutes. Refresh in cold water. Pull off the outer leaves and arrange these overlapping on a double thickness of cheesecloth to form a large circle. Squeeze out excess moisture from the remaining center leaves of the cabbage, chop them and put into a large bowl. Cut the sausage across at an angle into thin slices and add these to the cabbage.

Put the oil in a heavy-bottomed pan over low heat, add the onions, stir well and cook for 10 to 15 minutes or until translucent, taking care not to allow them to brown. Toward the end of this cooking, stir in the garlic. Transfer to the bowl with the cabbage.

In a dry pan and over the lowest heat, toast the cumin seeds peppercorns, mustard seeds and pepper flakes for 2 to 3 minutes, stirring. Then grind these to a powder and add to the stuffing mixture with the pork, fish sauce, bread crumbs, lemongrass, chopped parsley and the egg. Season lightly with salt and mix all together, starting with a fork and finishing with your hands to ensure an even distribution of all the elements. Make a small patty and fry it in a little oil. Taste this and adjust the seasoning of the mixture with more salt and pepper accordingly.

Form the stuffing into a ball and place in the center of the arranged cabbage leaves, then fold the leaves up and around to cover. Tie the cheesecloth tightly around it. Put into a pan into which it will fit comfortably and cover with the stock. Add some water if needed to cover and bring to a boil, skim and lower the heat, then simmer for 1¼ hours.

Remove the cabbage from the stock, drain in a colander and untie the cheesecloth. Transfer the stuffed cabbage to a cutting board and slice it into 8 wedges. Put a wedge in each of 8 warmed soup plates. Ladle over some of the cooking broth and snip over the chives.

rice noodle soup with tamarind, peanuts and pork

This dish is typical of street food to be found in Melbourne and Sydney. If you have a Chinatown near to you, you can buy the glazed Chinese barbecued pork (*char siu* in Cantonese) from delicatessens and some restaurants. The soup can also be made with duck.

6 cups chicken or pork stock
  (page 152)
3 tablespoons fish sauce
2 teaspoons Asian sesame oil
2-inch piece fresh ginger,
  juiced (page 144)
4 tablespoons tamarind water
  (page 157)
1 teaspoon sugar
½ teaspoon red pepper flakes
5 ounces Chinese barbecued
  pork (see above)
¾ cup roasted peanuts
6 ounces dried rice noodles
½ bunch fresh Chinese chives

to serve
2 red chilies, thinly sliced
3 to 4 ounces bean sprouts
1 lime, quartered lengthwise
more fish sauce

serves 4

Bring the stock to a gentle simmer and add the fish sauce, sesame oil and ginger juice.

At the same time, bring a large pan of water to a rapid boil. While it is heating, mix the tamarind water in a bowl with the sugar and pepper flakes. Carve the pork across the grain into 12 to 16 thin slices. Crush the roasted peanuts in a bag with a rolling pin.

Cook the noodles for 4 minutes in the pan of boiling water, then drain in a colander. Divide them among 4 large warmed bowls and arrange the pork slices on top. Ladle over the stock, and add 1 tablespoon of the chili tamarind sauce to each bowl. Scatter over a few whole chives, then top each bowl with 1 tablespoon of crushed nuts.

Serve the soup, offering the bean sprouts, sliced chilies, lime wedges, more fish sauce and the remaining crushed nuts in separate bowls at the table.

pumpkin, bean and greens soup

Young, tender cabbages, with their hearts not yet formed and their leaves imparting a slightly bitter intensity, are perfect for this robust soup, although cavolo nero (Italian black cabbage) or Swiss chard (both green and red) could be substituted.

⅓ cup dried flageolet, navy, or
  other small white beans
salt
1 small fennel bulb, diced
1 small yellow onion, diced
2 garlic cloves, finely chopped
1 celery stalk, diced, plus
  3 tablespoons chopped
  celery leaves
4 tablespoons olive oil
pepper
10-ounce piece pumpkin,
  peeled and cut into chunks
10 ounces greens (see above),
  coarsely chopped
1 tablespoon fresh
  thyme leaves
extra-virgin olive oil,
  to dress
grated Parmesan cheese,
  to serve (optional)

serves 4

The day before, put the beans to soak in cold water. Next day, rinse the beans and put them in a small saucepan. Cover with water, bring to a boil, then lower the heat to a simmer and cook for 20 minutes. Season lightly with ¼ teaspoon of salt, then continue to cook for a further 10 to 20 minutes, or until you judge them almost done. Remove from the heat and leave to cool in their cooking water.

In a large saucepan over a medium heat, cook the fennel, onion, garlic and diced celery in the olive oil for 3 to 4 minutes, stirring. Add 5 cups water, season with salt and pepper and bring to a boil. Lower the heat and simmer for 20 minutes. Then add the pumpkin, the greens and the beans with their cooking liquid. Simmer for 5 minutes, then add the celery leaves and thyme. Continue to cook for a further 5 minutes.

Ladle into large, shallow soup bowls. Drizzle extra-virgin olive oil on top and grind over some black pepper. Serve with a good rustic bread and, if you like, offer grated Parmesan at the table for people to add themselves.

ko-samui chicken, shrimp and coconut soup

Ko-samui is a small island off Thailand, the main cash crop of which, coconut, is also central to every area of activity, from housebuilding and cooking fires to making mats. This soup encapsulates all the key ingredients of the island's food culture, combining local seafood and meats with galangal, lemongrass and kaffir lime — all now everyday flavorings in Australian cooking.

7 ounces boneless, skinless
chicken breast

7 ounces snapper or other
firm-fleshed white fish fillets

8 large shrimp

3 lemongrass stalks

2-inch piece fresh galangal
(page 156)

1-inch piece fresh ginger

2 teaspoons sambal oelek
(page 157)

4 cups coconut milk

10 kaffir lime leaves

5 tablespoons fish sauce

juice of ½ lime

1 cup fresh cilantro leaves

1 cup fresh Thai basil leaves

serves 4

Cut the chicken into 1-inch cubes. Skin the fish fillets, if necessary, and cut into similar-sized cubes. Peel and devein the shrimp.

Peel off the outer tough leaf or leaves of the lemongrass, cut off the root stem and cut the stalk into 2-inch pieces. Cut the galangal and ginger into thin slices, and put all three flavorings in a pan with the sambal and about 1 cup cold water. Bring to a boil, turn down the heat and simmer for 5 minutes. Then add the coconut milk and lime leaves. Simmer for 10 minutes.

Add the chicken to the stock, together with the fish sauce and lime juice. After 2 minutes, add the fish and shrimp. Simmer these for a minute, then put in the cilantro and basil.

Serve at once in deep bowls, distributing the chicken, fish and shrimp before ladling over the broth. The lemongrass, galangal, ginger and lemongrass are also served for visual effect but not eaten.

salted salmon with tomato herb dressing

Light salting has an intriguing impact on the flavor of the cooked fish. In this recipe the salmon is salted in the refrigerator for 24 hours before being briefly poached, to be served warm with a tomato herb vinaigrette. This dish also makes an excellent main course, served with boiled new potatoes tossed with butter and chives.

1 salmon tail section, 2¼ pounds,
  cut from a whole fish
4 tablespoons sea salt

the poaching liquid:
2 celery stalks, thinly sliced
2 carrots, thinly sliced
4 lemons, quartered
⅔ cup champagne vinegar or
  white wine vinegar
1 bunch of fresh thyme sprigs
2 bay leaves
1 star anise

for the tomato herb dressing:
4 ripe plum (Roma) tomatoes
2 tablespoons finely chopped
  fresh cilantro
2 tablespoons finely chopped
  chives
2 tablespoons finely chopped
  fresh flat-leaf parsley
juice of 1 lemon
½ cup extra-virgin olive oil
salt and pepper

serves 4

The day before, put the ingredients for the poaching liquid in a fish poacher or pan with the fish. This helps you use to assess precisely the right amount of water. Pour over just enough to cover the fish by 1 inch. Remove the fish, pat dry and reserve. Bring the liquid to a boil. Lower the heat and simmer for 30 minutes. Turn off the heat and leave to cool.

Cut a shallow crosshatch into the skin of the fish with a very sharp knife, or better still, a scalpel. (Scalpels with disposable blades can be bought from stationers and have many uses in the kitchen. Between uses, stick the blade into a cork to keep it safely.) Cut only just through the skin and not deep into the fish. The aim is just to assist the penetration of the salt into the flesh. Scatter half the sea salt on a sheet of plastic wrap large enough to wrap the fish and lay it on top. Press the remaining salt into the other side and wrap tightly, put into a dish and refrigerate for 24 hours.

Next day, make the dressing: blanch the tomatoes in boiling water for 30 seconds, refresh in cold water and peel. Cut into quarters and remove the seeds and surrounding pulp and discard. Cut the flesh into small dice. Combine with the herbs, lemon juice, oil and salt and pepper.

Bring the poaching liquid to a boil in the fish poacher. Rinse the fish and put it in the boiling poaching liquid. Bring it back to a boil and immediately lower the heat to a bare simmer. Poach for 8 minutes. Remove the salmon and transfer to a cutting board, using the rack if cooking in a fish poacher or with 2 slotted spatulas, to avoid breaking the fish.

Remove the skin from the top half of the salmon. Run a large knife down the central line cutting down to the spine, then gently slide the knife laterally between the bones and the flesh to remove as 2 fillets. Put these on warmed serving plates, lift the bones away, and repeat with the 2 remaining fillets.

Stir the dressing and spoon it over the salmon fillets. Serve at once.

rock oysters with red onion salsa

Australians are great oyster consumers and the country is blessed with an enviable supply of Pacific rock oysters. These are usually sold ready-opened by Australian fishmongers, which is fine if you are going to rush home and eat them at once. Bought unopened from your fishmonger or by mail order, surrounded with seaweed or a damp cloth, they will stay alive in the refrigerator for several days, and they really are not that difficult to open.

Salsa, the simplest and most popular of Mexican sauces, combines peeled and diced raw ripe tomato with onion, hot chili and aromatic cilantro. It can be served with pretty much anything as a clean-tasting relish, and is called different things by different people — salsa cruda, salsa fresca, salsa Mexicana. The important thing is the ripeness and intensity of flavor of the tomatoes. Unless buying vine-ripened tomatoes in season, always leave them to ripen at room temperature. Plum tomatoes generally have the best flavor and a sunny windowsill is an ideal place to allow them to develop the necessary sweet intensity over three or four days.

Salsa and oysters form a felicitous partnership of tastes and textures. Ideally, prepare the salsa 30 to 45 minutes before you eat it. This gives sufficient time for the flavors to mingle. If left longer than an hour, water exudes from the tomatoes and onion, giving a watery finish, while the cilantro becomes limp and loses its aroma.

First make the salsa: core the tomatoes with a small sharp knife and cut a small cross on the opposite ends to help peeling. Blanch them in boiling water for 10 to 15 seconds, then transfer immediately to a bowl of ice water and leave for 1 minute. Remove, peel and cut into quarters. Scoop out the seeds and pulp and discard (or add to a stock). Cut the flesh into small dice and set aside.

Cut the onion into similar-sized dice. Cut off the stem from the chili, cut in half and scrape out the seeds and discard. Chop the chili finely and the cilantro leaves coarsely. Add to the tomatoes with the lime juice and olive oil. Season with pepper, stir and leave to stand while you open the oysters.

24 oysters
for the red onion salsa:
6 ripe plum (Roma) tomatoes
2 small red onions, peeled
2 red chilies
½ cup fresh cilantro leaves
2 tablespoons lime juice
2 tablespoons olive oil
pepper

Put each well-scrubbed oyster on a flat surface with the flatter shell upward and hinged end toward you. Hold the other end firmly in a cloth with one hand and ease the tip of a knife into the small opening in the hinge with the other. Wiggle the tip until the muscle gives. Once inserted, twist the knife to lever open, taking care not to let any shell fragments fall on the flesh. Sever the muscle attaching the oyster to the shell.

Arrange the opened oysters on a plate of crushed ice and put a spoonful of salsa on each.

serves 4

vinegared crab and green papaya salad

Crab is cooked in exactly the same way as lobster (page 56). As soon as the crab is cool enough to handle, position it back downward and twist off the claws and legs. Crack the claws open with the back of a heavy knife and extract the flesh. Pull away the small pincer to remove the blade bone and discard. A gentle but firm pull from the larger pincer will bring away the tip concealed inside. The legs have a much softer shell, but are a little difficult to deal with.

Give the tail flap a knock to loosen it, and then use a screwdriver — or something else that won't snap — to lever out the underside panel. Lift it up to pull away the bony central section that contains most of the white meat. Behind the mouth you will find the stomach sac and intestinal bits, which you discard. Remove the translucent gills that are curled over the bony central section and discard these also. Use a small spoon to scrape out the brown flesh from the outer sections of the shell. Make two cuts down and through the bony central section in a V to give you four accessible planes, and use a thin metal pick or skewer to extract all the meat concealed in the little pockets and tunnels.

Turn the crab the other way up and scrape out the remaining white flesh from the leg sockets. You now have the prime white and red claw meat, ivory shell meat and brown meat, which includes the liver. This recipe only uses the white meat.

Green or unripe papaya is sold by both Asian and West Indian grocers. If unobtainable, sour green mangoes may be substituted.

1 green papaya, about 10 ounces, peeled
1 daikon, about 10 ounces, peeled
about 3 large carrots, peeled
1 teaspoon salt
14 ounces fresh cooked white crabmeat

for the pickling liquid:
3 tablespoons Japanese rice vinegar (page 157)
1 packet (¼ ounce) of instant dashi (page 156)
2 teaspoons superfine sugar
½ teaspoon ginger juice (page 144)

serves 4

Put all the pickling liquid ingredients except the ginger juice in a pan and bring to a boil. Remove from the heat and leave to cool, then add the ginger juice.

Cut the papaya in half lengthwise and remove the seeds. Slice the papaya, daikon and carrot into long, thin strips on a mandoline or with a potato peeler. Put all of them together in a large bowl. Sprinkle with the salt and leave to stand for 5 to 10 minutes, then gently mix together.

Remove the vegetable strips from the bowl, shaking off any liquid, and put them on paper towels to dry. Wipe out the bowl and return the dried strips to it, then pour over the pickling liquid. Leave to marinate for 1 hour, tossing from time to time.

Using a slotted spoon, lift out the pickled vegetables and divide among 4 shallow bowls, stacking them as high as you can. Scatter over the crabmeat and dress each mound with 1 tablespoon of the pickling liquid.

thai mussels with coriander

Farmed mussels are of a uniform size, strictly quality-controlled and excellent value. They really are the cook's friend, as they can be prepared in advance, keep in the refrigerator for a couple of days and cook in minutes. Sweet chili sauce, *saus prik* in Thai, is the traditional accompaniment to shrimp rolls, fried chicken and cold meats. Sold bottled as "all-purpose" sauce, the sweetness comes from pineapple juice and red plums.

4½ pounds mussels
⅔ cup Thai sweet chili sauce
1 teaspoon fish sauce
2 ounces fresh cilantro sprigs
  with roots, finely chopped

serves 4

Debeard, scrape and wash the mussels, discarding any that do not close when tapped. Rinse in a colander under cold running water for 2 to 3 minutes. Leave to drain.

Put a large pan with a close-fitting lid over high heat. When very hot, add the chili and fish sauces, then the mussels all at once. Stir, put on the lid and steam for about 4 minutes, shaking from time to time. They should all have opened. If not, give them another 30 seconds. Add the cilantro and toss. Remove from the heat and replace the lid for a minute or two. Discard any which stubbornly refuse to open.

Serve in large warmed soup bowls, piling the mussels as high as you can and spooning the spicy cooking liquid over.

salt and pepper squid with arugula

6 cups corn oil
6 tablespoons all-purpose flour
2 teaspoons white pepper
2 teaspoons salt
14 ounces cleaned squid tubes
1 lemon, quartered, to serve

for the arugula salad:
4 tablespoons mayonnaise
1 teaspoon lemon juice
pepper
7 ounces arugula

serves 4

First prepare the salad: in a bowl, whisk the mayonnaise with 1 tablespoon of water and the lemon juice. Season with a few turns of black pepper. Toss the arugula leaves in this dressing to coat and mound on 4 plates.

In a deep fryer or other deep pan, heat the oil to 375°F. Sieve the flour, white pepper and salt together into a bowl. Cut the squid tubes across into thin rings and dry on paper towels.

Toss the squid rings in the seasoned flour to coat, shaking off any excess and place in a frying basket. Plunge into the hot oil and fry for 1 minute, when the squid will be crisp and golden brown. Drain on paper towels and divide among the 4 plates, placing on top of the arugula. Serve immediately with a lemon quarter on the side.

grilled scallops with black bean sauce and cilantro

You will need to look for scallops still in the shell for this recipe. When buying them, ask for ones with 3-inch shells, giving you 5 scallops to a generous portion. Have them opened and cleaned but left attached to the base of the shell.

20 scallops (see above)
olive oil, for brushing
pepper
2 cups fresh cilantro leaves

for the black bean sauce:
3 tablespoons dried black beans
  (page 156)
1 tablespoon sunflower oil
½ small yellow onion,
  finely chopped
1-inch piece of fresh ginger,
  peeled and finely chopped
4 small garlic cloves, finely
  chopped
1 cup shrimp stock (page 153)
1 tablespoon Chinese rice wine
  or medium-sweet sherry
3 tablespoons soy sauce
2½ teaspoons superfine sugar
1 teaspoon cornstarch

serves 4

First, make the sauce: soak the beans overnight in ½ cup water. Drain.

In a saucepan, heat the oil over medium heat and cook the onion, ginger and garlic for 2 minutes. Add the black beans, stock, rice wine or sherry, soy sauce and sugar. Bring to a simmer and cook for 30 seconds.

Mix the cornstarch to a paste with 1 tablespoon of water and add slowly to the bean mixture, stirring. The thickening effect will be instantaneous, but continue to cook for 3 to 4 minutes. Keep warm.

Meanwhile, preheat a broiler.

Put the scallops on a baking sheet. Brush with olive oil and season with pepper, then broil for 4 to 5 minutes, or until just cooked. The scallops are cooked when the flesh takes on color and the texture is firm to the touch, while the interior is still moist and tender.

Put the scallops on 4 warmed plates, spooning a little black bean sauce on each. Scatter over the cilantro leaves and serve at once.

shrimp risotto with ikan bilis

Ikan bilis, very small salted and dried fish similar to smelt (also known as whitebait), are eaten as a part of a traditional Malay breakfast.

6 cups shrimp or vegetable stock
 (page153)
5 ounces shrimp, peeled and
 deveined
3 tablespoons sunflower oil
1 ounce ikan bilis (see
 above and page 156)
3 tablespoons butter
1 tablespoon olive oil
4 shallots, finely chopped
2 garlic cloves, finely chopped
1 cup finely diced fennel
1 cup Arborio rice
⅞ cup dry white wine
½ cup cilantro leaves, finely
 shredded

serves 4

Put the stock in a saucepan and bring to a boil, then reduce to a bare simmer. While it is heating, cut the shrimp into ½-inch pieces.

Put the sunflower oil in a wok over medium heat and, when it is hot, add the ikan bilis and fry until golden brown. Remove and drain on paper towels.

In a heavy-bottomed saucepan over medium heat, melt 2 tablespoons of the butter with the olive oil. Add the shallots, garlic and fennel and cook gently for 1 to 2 minutes, or until soft and translucent, taking care not to allow them to color.

Add the rice and stir for 1 to 2 minutes to coat, giving it a clear and shiny appearance. Pour in the wine and stir until it is absorbed. Then add a first ladleful of hot stock, stirring until it is all absorbed. Repeat this process for the next 20 to 25 minutes, or until all the stock is used and your risotto has taken on the characteristic consistency of creamy porridge, but with the individual grains of rice still retaining a residual bite.

In a small pan over medium heat, melt the remaining 1 tablespoon butter and add the shrimp pieces. Sauté gently for 1 minute to cook them through without coloring them, then stir them into the risotto.

Serve in 4 warmed soup plates, mounding the risotto in the middle. Scatter over the ikan bilis, followed by the shredded cilantro and serve at once.

shrimp summer rolls

These are very fashionable at the moment since, unlike most Southeast Asian or Chinese wrappers, rice wrappers do not need to be cooked and the finished product is thus low in calories. Vietnamese in origin, you can buy them from Southeast Asian markets. They are available in differently sized rounds, ranging from 6 inches to 12 inches across. All you do is slide the hard, flat translucent wrappers through a bowl of hot water and they soften and become slightly opaque. You then fill them with whatever takes your fancy, roll them up and serve them, usually with a thin, spicy dipping sauce.

8 round rice wrappers, each 8½
  inches across
1 tablespoon fish sauce
8 ounces bean sprouts
4 ounces oyster mushrooms,
  thinly sliced
16 fresh mint leaves
handful of fresh cilantro leaves
1 pound shrimp, cooked in
  boiling water, drained, peeled
  and sliced in half lengthwise

for the dipping sauce:
2 teaspoons superfine sugar
4 tablespoons rice vinegar
1 tablespoon sambal oelek (page
  157)
handful of fresh cilantro leaves
1 tablespoon fish sauce
⅔ cup peanut or sunflower oil
salt and pepper

serves 4

First, make the dipping sauce: mix the sugar with the rice vinegar until dissolved and put in a food processor. Fry the sambal for 2 to 3 minutes and add to the processor together with the cilantro, the fish sauce and the peanut or sunflower oil. Blitz to a homogenized sauce. Taste and season.

Mix the mushrooms with the bean sprouts.

Pass each wrapper through a bowl of hot water and put it on a board. Brush the middle with a little fish sauce, leaving a border. In a bowl, mix the bean sprouts with the mushroom slices. Arrange one-eighth of the mixture down the center of each round. Add 2 mint leaves and some whole cilantro leaves to each. Distribute the sliced shrimp on top. Fold the lower third of each wrapper up over the filling, then roll from one side to the other to form a cylinder. If not serving immediately, put on a tray lined with a damp cloth and place another damp cloth on top to prevent them drying out.

Serve at once with the dipping sauce, or keep in the refrigerator covered as described for up to 2 hours.

chicken salad with anchovy and capers

4 cups chicken stock (page 152)
4 boneless, skinless chicken
   breast halves
2 ounces canned tuna in
   olive oil, drained
4 anchovy fillets in olive oil,
   drained
⅞ cup mayonnaise
2 teaspoons lemon juice
salt and pepper
1 head frisée, separated
   into leaves
1 tablespoon extra-virgin
   olive oil
2 tablespoons small capers,
   drained

serves 4

Bring the stock to a boil in a pan. Add the chicken breasts, turn the heat down and simmer for 7 to 8 minutes. Turn off the heat and leave the chicken to cool in the stock.

When chicken has cooled, put the tuna and anchovies in a blender or food processor. Add the mayonnaise and 3 tablespoons of the stock and blitz for a minute, or until you have a smooth sauce with the consistency of pourable cream. Add 1 teaspoon of the lemon juice, season with salt and pepper and reserve.

Take the chicken out of the stock and pat dry with paper towels, then cut it into long, thin slices. Put in a large bowl and toss with the sauce.

In another bowl, toss the frisée with the olive oil, the remaining lemon juice and some pepper.

Mound the frisée in the middle of 4 plates and arrange the sliced chicken on top. Scatter over the capers. Finish by drizzling a little more of the tuna sauce on top and grinding over some more pepper.

chicken and shrimp salad with garlic croutons

Chicken and shrimp are often featured together in Spanish cooking. Here they are combined in a salad inspired by gazpacho soup.

8 ounces cooked boneless,
   skinless chicken breast, cut into
   ½-inch cubes
8 ounces peeled cooked shrimp
2 pounds ripe plum (Roma)
   tomatoes
1 red onion
1 garlic clove
2 tablespoons balsamic vinegar
salt and pepper

Use a breast from a cold roast chicken or cook a breast slowly in a nonstick pan with a little olive oil. Buy ready-cooked shrimp or poach them in their shells in well-salted, simmering water for 1 minute if small, or 2 to 3 minutes if large. Refresh briefly in ice water, drain and refrigerate until needed (up to 12 hours).

At least 4 hours before you plan to serve: core the tomatoes, cut a cross in the stem ends, scald in boiling water for 30 seconds, refresh in ice water and peel. Cut into quarters, stripping out and discarding seeds. Put half of the quarters in a food processor with one-quarter

1 cucumber
1 red pepper, oven-roasted and
  peeled (page 88)
½ cup extra-virgin olive oil
½ cup fresh basil leaves

for the garlic croutons:
2 garlic cloves, finely chopped
4 tablespoons olive oil
¼ teaspoon red pepper flakes
2 slices of white bread, crusts
  removed and cut into cubes

serves 4

of the onion, coarsely chopped, and the garlic. Add the vinegar, ½
teaspoon salt and ¼ teaspoon pepper. Blitz to a purée and pour into a
bowl.

Cut the cucumber into ½-inch dice and the bell pepper into ½-inch
squares. Stir these into the purée, together with the remaining tomato
quarters. Adjust the seasoning. Refrigerate for 4 to 12 hours.

Cut the remaining red onion into ½-inch dice. Stir this into the salad,
together with the chicken and shrimp and the olive oil.

Make the croutons: put a dry nonstick frying pan over low heat. Put
the garlic into a bowl with the oil. Season and add the pepper flakes.
Stir to mix, then add the bread cubes and toss to coat. Transfer to the
pan and cook slowly, tossing and turning, until crisp and brown.

Spoon the salad into soup plates. Scatter over croutons and finish with
torn basil leaves and more coarsely ground pepper. Serve immediately.

fried egg noodles with fish cake, chicken and thai basil

14 ounces thin Chinese egg
  noodles
2 boneless, skinless chicken
  breast halves
2 red shallots
2 garlic cloves
4 tablespoons sunflower oil
2 tablespoons sambal oelek (page
  157)
½ cup fresh Thai basil leaves
1 packet fish cake, 5½ ounces,
  thinly sliced
8 green onions, trimmed and cut
  into ¾-inch pieces
7 ounces bean sprouts
4 tablespoons fish sauce
2 green chilies, thinly sliced

serves 4

Put the noodles in a large heatproof bowl, pour boiling water over
them and leave to stand for 1 minute, then drain. Cut the chicken
breast across into thin strips. Finely chop the shallots and garlic.

Put a wok over high heat, then add the oil and heat until almost
smoking. Stir-fry the chicken strips until golden brown, remove and
reserve. Add the shallots and garlic, lower the heat and stir-fry until
soft. Stir in the sambal and cook for 1 minute, then add the Thai basil,
chicken strips and sliced fish cake, tossing and stirring constantly. Add
in the green onions, the bean sprouts and noodles, then season with
the fish sauce.

Serve in a large warmed bowl, making sure all the elements are well
combined. Offer the green chilies in a small bowl on the side.

spaghetti with sardines, capers and parsley

It's the grilling of the sardines in this dish that imparts such a good flavor.

8 large sardines, cleaned
  and gutted
sea salt and pepper
1 pound spaghetti
4 tablespoons extra-virgin
  olive oil
2 small garlic cloves
2 tablespoons baby capers
2 tablespoons coarsely chopped
  fresh flat-leaf parsley

serves 4

Put a saucepan with 4 quarts of salted water to boil. Rinse the sardines under running water and dry on paper towels. Crush some sea salt and sprinkle it over the fish with some milled pepper. Heat a dry ridged grill pan over high heat until smoking hot.

Grill the fish for 2 minutes, or until the skin is charred and crisp. Turn and give the other side 2 minutes also. Transfer to a large plate to cool.

When the water is boiling rapidly, add the spaghetti and cook for the time specified on the package, or until just al dente.

While the spaghetti is cooking, use a small knife to lift the sardine flesh from the bones, separating from head and tail in the largest pieces you can manage.

Put the oil in a small saucepan over a low heat. Coarsely chop the garlic and stir it into the oil. Cook gently, allowing the flavor to infuse, then stir in the capers and parsley. Season with pepper and remove the pan from the heat.

When you judge the spaghetti to be done, drain in a large colander and return to the hot saucepan. Pour over the sauce, toss together and add the pieces of sardine.

Divide among 4 warmed shallow pasta bowls and serve.

fried vermicelli noodles with chicken and shrimp

1 egg
salt and pepper
2 small green chilies
about 4 tablespoons fish sauce
2 garlic cloves
3 small shallots
3 tablespoons dried shrimp
  (page 156), soaked in warm
  water for 10 minutes and
  drained
3 tablespoons sunflower or
  peanut oil
5 ounces boneless, skinless
  chicken breast, thinly sliced
3 tablespoons sambal oelek (page
  157)
3 to 4 cabbage leaves,
  thinly sliced
5 ounces peeled cooked shrimp
1 small bunch fresh Chinese
  chives, cut into 1-inch pieces
12 ounces dried fine rice
  vermicelli (fine rice sticks),
  soaked in cold water for
  1 hour and drained
4 iceberg lettuce leaves, rolled
  and shredded
1/2 cup crispy fried shallots
  (page 13)
2 lemons, cut into wedges,
  to serve

serves 4

Preheat a nonstick pan over medium heat. Break the egg into a small bowl and beat lightly with a fork. Season with salt and pepper and pour into the pan. Allow just to set, then turn over and remove from the pan. Roll it up into a cigar shape. When cool, cut it across into thin rings and reserve.

Thinly slice the chilies, put them in a small bowl with 1 tablespoon of the fish sauce and reserve.

In a blender or food processor, blend to a paste the garlic, shallots and dried shrimps with 2 tablespoons water.

Put the oil in a wok over medium-to-high heat and fry the paste for about a minute, when it will give off a heady fragrance. Add the chicken and sambal oelek and continue to fry until the chicken is just done.

Add the cabbage, then 30 seconds later the cooked shrimp and chives, followed by the noodles. Keep tossing and turning to mix all the ingredients together, then add the remaining 3 tablespoons fish sauce. Taste for seasoning and if you feel it needs it, add another splash of fish sauce.

Transfer to a large shallow serving dish and scatter the shredded lettuce over, followed by the sliced omelet. Sprinkle over the crispy shallots and serve at once, with the bowl of sliced green chilies in fish sauce and the lemon wedges for those people who want a little extra heat or sharpness to help themselves.

garlic roast chicken salad with tabbouleh

Tabbouleh is a salad made from bulgur, wheat that has been steamed, dried and then ground. The salad was originally Lebanese and is characterized by its green color, the result of using lots of herbs.

1 head garlic
salt and pepper
1 free-range chicken,
 about 3 pounds
1 cup fresh cilantro
 leaves and stems
1 cup fresh flat-leaf parsley
 leaves and stems
extra-virgin olive oil for brushing
 and dressing, plus $^1/_2$ cup
¾ cup bulgur
1 Lebanese-type cucumber
 (page 156)
8 green onions, thinly sliced
1 lemon
1 Savoy cabbage, cored and outer
 leaves removed

serves 4

The day before or several hours ahead, preheat the oven to 475°F and prepare the chicken. Separate the garlic cloves and peel them, then bruise them by thumping them hard with the heel of your hand. Season them with salt and pepper and put them into the chicken cavity together with the stems from the cilantro and parsley. Brush the bird all over with olive oil and season generously.

Put the bird breast side down on a rack and roast for 15 minutes. Turn it breast side up, lower the temperature to 400°F and cook for a further 40 minutes. Remove and leave to cool.

Cut the legs off the chicken and remove the meat from the bones. Remove the breasts whole and carve these across into thick slices.

Rinse the bulgur in a sieve under cold running water until the water runs clear. Put it into a large bowl of cold water and leave to soak for 1 hour. Cut half the cucumber into small dice and put the pieces into a colander. Sprinkle with salt and leave to drain. Then cover with cold water and leave for 30 minutes to drain.

Transfer the bulgur to a sieve and press to extract as much moisture as you can. Return it to the bowl and add the green onions. Put the diced cucumber into a clean cloth and squeeze to extract as much water as possible, then stir it into the bulgur. Pull off and reserve for garnish some whole leaves from the parsley and cilantro and finely chop the rest. Add to the bulgur. Add the $^1/_2$ cup olive oil and the juice and zest of the lemon. Season well and stir all together with a fork. Taste. It may benefit from some more lemon juice and perhaps more oil.

While the bulgur is soaking, put on a large pan of salted boiling water to boil. Blanch 12 of the best inner cabbage leaves for 2 to 3 minutes. Transfer to a bowl of ice water for a minute. Drain in a colander and then pat dry with paper towels. Arrange 3 of the cabbage leaves to cover the center of each plate. Mound the tabbouleh on top, then arrange the chicken over it. Scatter over the reserved cilantro and parsley. Cut the remaining cucumber in long strips with a potato peeler and scatter over the salad. Dress with olive oil and grind over some pepper just before serving.

crispy fried chicken wings with peanut and tamarind sauce

As the wings are fried in oil, it is a good idea to trim off as much fat as possible. This also helps the absorption of flavor from the turmeric. You can fry in a wok or in an electric frying pan set to 375°F.

12 to 16 chicken wings,
 depending on size
1 teaspoon turmeric
salt
½ cup sunflower oil

for the peanut and tamarind sauce:
2 or 3 dried red chilies
1⅓ cups raw peanuts
1 tablespoon tamarind pulp
 (page 157)
¼-inch piece fresh galangal
 (page 156), peeled
1 stalk of lemongrass, outer
 leaves removed and thinly
 sliced
4 red shallots, sliced
3½ tablespoons sunflower oil
scant 2 tablespoons
 superfine sugar

serves 4

Trim the chicken wings and put them in a large bowl. Mix together the turmeric and ½ teaspoon of salt and rub this into the wings. Leave them to absorb the seasoning for 30 minutes at room temperature.

Prepare the chilies for the sauce: put them in a bowl, pour over boiling water and leave them to soak for 15 minutes.

Preheat the oven to 400°F. Put the peanuts on a baking sheet and roast them until golden brown.

While the nuts are browning, in a bowl dissolve the tamarind pulp in 2 tablespoons of water, rubbing it between your fingers. Pass this through a fine sieve into another bowl, pressing with a wooden spoon. Reserve this tamarind juice, discarding the pulp.

Remove the peanuts from the oven and, when cool enough to handle, rub them between your hands to rid them of their skins and put into a food processor. Blitz to a fine crumb, transfer to a bowl and reserve.

Drain the chilies and chop them coarsely with their seeds. Put in the food processor and work to a purée. Scrape into another bowl. Put the galangal, lemongrass and sliced shallots in the food processor and work until uniformly crushed and blended.

Preheat the oil in the wok or pan. Fry 4 to 6 chicken wings at a time for 4 to 6 minutes, until crisp and golden brown. Transfer each batch to a baking sheet lined with paper towels and keep warm in a low oven.

While the last batch is cooking, put the sunflower oil for the sauce in a pan or wok over medium-to-high heat and, when hot, add the chili purée and stir-fry for 30 seconds. Add the galangal mixture and continue to stir for another 30 seconds. Then add the tamarind juice, 2 tablespoons of water, the ground peanuts, the sugar and salt. Bring to a boil, lower the heat and simmer for 2 to 3 minutes.

Serve the sauce in individual small bowls in which to dip the wings.

frittata with ham hock, goats' cheese, artichoke and herbs

Frittatas can be as light and simple or as substantial and complex as you care to make them. The only absolute is that the eggs for this essentially Italian omelet should be completely fresh and free-range, or it will lack flavor. If Jerusalem artichokes are unavailable, you can use artichoke hearts bottled in olive oil.

1 ham hock or shank
4 or 5 Jerusalem artichokes
  juice of 1 lemon
8 free-range eggs
salt and pepper
1 tablespoon coarsely chopped
  fresh flat-leaf parsley
½ teaspoon fresh thyme leaves
2 tablespoons olive oil
5 ounces fresh goat cheese, cut
  into small cubes
arugula leaves, to serve

serves 4

Put the hock or shank in a large saucepan, cover with cold water and bring to a boil. Lower the heat and simmer for 1 hour. Leave to cool in the water. Using a small knife and your hands, remove the skin and discard. Separate the meat from the bones and cut it into 1-inch pieces.

Peel the artichokes, putting them in a bowl of cold water acidulated with the lemon juice to prevent discoloration. Drain, rinse and transfer to a pan. Cover with water, add salt and bring to a boil. Lower the heat and simmer for 20 minutes, or until tender. Drain well and, when cool enough to handle, cut into slices.

Preheat the broiler or the oven to 425°F.

Break the eggs into a large mixing bowl and beat them lightly. Season (being careful with the salt as both the cheese and the ham are already salty) and add the herbs.

Put a heavy cast-iron or heatproof nonstick frying pan over medium heat and, when hot, add the oil and tilt the pan to cover the entire base. Pour in the egg mixture and leave for 1 minute, then reduce the heat slightly. Cook for another minute, then scatter on the ham, cheese and artichokes. Continue to cook until almost set. Transfer to under the broiler or into the oven for a few minutes to finish.

As soon as you deem the center to be done (it should be set but still moist), remove and leave to cool for 2 to 3 minutes. Put a large flat plate or chopping board on the top of the pan and invert both simultaneously to turn out the frittata.

Serve cut in wedges, with some arugula on the side.

deep-fried pork wontons with cilantro chutney

Wonton wrappers, usually used to make poached dumplings, deep-fry perfectly, puffing up to make a crisp and crunchy covering for the filling. The cilantro chutney makes a cold fresh-tasting contrast.

1 teaspoon coriander seeds
1 cup diced onion
1 garlic clove, diced
1 small bunch fresh chives,
  chopped
½ teaspoon red pepper flakes
12 ounces ground pork
salt and pepper
20 wonton wrappers

for the cilantro chutney:
2 ounces fresh cilantro sprigs
2 tablespoons grated coconut
  (page 156)
1 tablespoon rice vinegar
1 hot green chili
1 tablespoon lemon juice
⅔ cup thick yogurt
1 teaspoon cumin seeds

serves 4

Toast the coriander seeds in a dry pan over a low heat for 3 to 4 minutes. Grind to a powder and put in a food processor with the onion and garlic, the chives, the chili and the pork. Season with salt and pepper. Blitz to a coherent mass. Take out a spoonful, make into a patty, fry and eat to assess the seasoning. Adjust to taste.

Brush the edges of a wonton wrapper with a little water. Put a heaped teaspoon of the mixture in the middle, draw up opposite corners and pinch them together. Pull up the other two and pinch together, pinching the open edges together on both sides. Put on a lightly floured tray and cover with a cloth. Repeat with the remaining wrappers and filling. When completed, the wontons can be held in the refrigerator for 1 hour. Any longer and the moisture of the filling will cause the wrappers to stick to the tray and they will tear when you try to lift them off.

Make the cilantro chutney: chop the leaves and stalks coarsely and put in a food processor with the grated coconut, rice vinegar, chili and lemon juice. Blitz to a uniform green paste. Stir this paste into the yogurt. Add salt and pepper to taste.

Preheat a deep-fryer to 375°F. Cook the wontons in 2 batches, turning them with a slotted spoon to ensure even cooking, for about 4 to 5 minutes, until crisp and golden brown all over. Drain on paper towels.

While the wontons are frying, toast the cumin seeds in a dry pan over a low heat for 3 minutes and scatter these on the top of the chutney. Serve the wontons as soon as all are cooked, with the chutney.

goat's milk feta with roast tomatoes, herbs and olive oil

Follow this combination with an arugula salad and you have a fine light summer lunch. Mass-produced cow's milk feta is now universally available in supermarkets, but it is worth going to a specialist cheese shop for goat's milk feta, which is vastly superior in both flavor and texture.

The roast tomatoes that accompany the cheese are best made the same day you plan to eat them, but they may be made a day or two before and stored in the refrigerator. If you do this, remove them in plenty of time to allow them come to room temperature before serving.

10 ounces goat's milk feta
½ cup olive oil
2 garlic cloves, sliced
2 fresh rosemary sprigs
2 fresh thyme sprigs
2 bay leaves
loaf of crusty bread, to serve

for the roast tomatoes:
2 ounces mixed fresh herb
  sprigs, such as basil, thyme,
  parsley, oregano and sage
1⅛ pounds ripe plum (Roma)
  tomatoes
salt and pepper

serves 4

Several days ahead: cut the feta into 4 equal pieces and place in a bowl with the oil, garlic, rosemary, thyme and bay leaves. Toss to coat and leave to marinate in the refrigerator for 2 to 3 days.

To roast the tomatoes: preheat an oven to 475°F.

Scatter half the herbs into a shallow roasting pan. Remove the cores from the tomatoes with a small knife and cut each in half lengthwise. Place these halves on top of the herbs, cut side up. Sprinkle over ¼ teaspoon of salt and grind over some pepper, then scatter over the remaining herbs. Roast for 15 minutes, then turn the oven down to 300°F and cook for a further 2 hours. Allow to cool. Remove the tomatoes, leaving the herbs behind.

To serve, divide the roasted tomato halves among 4 plates. Put a slice of feta next to them and drizzle over a little of the oil in which the cheese was marinated. Grind over some black pepper and serve with crusty bread.

parmesan and ricotta gratins with buttered spinach

Here individual cheese soufflés have a preliminary cooking in a water bath and are then turned out and returned to the oven briefly to achieve the required gratin finish.

melted butter for the molds, plus
  2 tablespoons
1¼ cups milk
3 tablespoons all-purpose flour
3 eggs, separated
scant ½ cup ricotta cheese
1¼ cups coarsely grated
  Parmesan cheese
⅔ cup light cream
salt and pepper

for the buttered spinach:
2 tablespoons butter
7 ounces spinach leaves
salt and pepper

serves 4

Preheat the oven to 350°F. Butter 4 small soufflé molds by coating the insides with a little melted butter. Stand them in a pan or dish and fill the pan or dish with water to come halfway up the sides of the molds. Remove the molds.

Put the milk in a small pan and bring to a boil. Turn off the heat and set aside. In a second saucepan, melt the 2 tablespoons butter over gentle heat. Stir in the flour to make a roux, cook for a minute or two, stirring. Then beat in the milk, a little at a time, until fully and smoothly incorporated. Cook gently for 20 minutes, stirring frequently to prevent sticking and burning. Remove from the heat and allow to cool. Beat in 2 of the egg yolks, then the ricotta and two-thirds of the Parmesan.

Whisk the egg whites until they form soft peaks. Fold 1 or 2 spoonfuls of the whites into the sauce and blend them in well. Add the sauce to the remaining whites and fold in gently to achieve the lightest amalgamation you can.

Divide the mixture among the molds, stand them in the water bath and bake for 1¼ hours. Remove them from the oven and leave to cool to room temperature, keeping the oven on.

In a bowl, whisk the remaining egg yolk and the cream together. Season with salt and pepper and set aside. Turn the soufflés out onto an ovenproof plate. Pour the cream mixture over them, sprinkle liberally with the remaining Parmesan and return to the oven for 5 minutes.

While they are finishing, cook the spinach: melt the butter in a wok or large frying pan over medium heat. Add the spinach, season with salt and pepper, and wilt the leaves for a minute. Drain in a colander.

The gratins should now be a dark, golden color and be ready to serve. Using a spatula, transfer them one at a time to warmed plates. Apportion the spinach around them and serve.

jerusalem artichoke and parmesan tart

Jerusalem artichokes, all too often relegated to soup, lend themselves to many more interesting treatments. In this smooth custard, they contrast pleasingly with the freshly grated Parmesan and crisp cheese pastry. Never use vinegar to acidulate the water in this dish as its strong flavor will impinge on the flavor of the finished tart.

1 1/8 pounds (peeled weight)
  Jerusalem artichokes (about 1 1/2
  pounds unpeeled)
juice of 1 lemon
salt
1 1/4 cups milk
1 3/4 cups heavy cream
3 whole eggs, plus 2 extra
  yolks
extra-virgin olive oil, to dress
1 piece Parmesan
  cheese, 2 to 3 ounces
pepper

for the cream cheese and
  Parmesan pastry:
1/2 cup cream cheese
5 tablespoons unsalted butter
2/3 cup all-purpose flour
2/3 cup self-rising flour
3 tablespoons grated
  Parmesan cheese

serves 10

Well ahead of time, remove the cream cheese and butter for the pastry from the refrigerator and allow to soften at room temperature.

Peel the artichokes, putting them in a bowl of cold water acidulated with the lemon juice to prevent discoloration. Drain, rinse and transfer to a pan. Cover with the milk and an equal amount of water, add salt and bring to a boil. Lower the heat and simmer for 20 minutes, or until tender.

While the artichokes are cooking, make the pastry: sift the flours into a bowl, add the cheeses and butter and rub together until you have a coarse bread crumb texture. Add about 1 1/2 tablespoons of cold water and form gently into a ball. Roll out and use to line a 10-inch tart pan. Leave to rest for 20 minutes.

Preheat the oven to 400°F.

Drain the cooked artichokes through a colander and leave to dry for 2 minutes. Put them into a food processor and blitz at full speed, pouring in half the cream through the feeder tube. Leave to cool and then season with salt and pepper. With the processor running, add the eggs with the extra yolks and the rest of the cream. Pass through a sieve into a pitcher and reserve.

Line the tart shell with parchment paper or foil, weight with dried beans and bake blind for 10 minutes. Turn the oven down to 300°F. Pour the custard into the tart shell and bake for 50 minutes. Remove and allow to cool for 3 to 5 minutes.

Preheat a broiler and, when hot, put the tart under and allow to color, watching it carefully all the time. It should brown, not burn.

Cut the tart into slices and serve on warmed plates. Drizzle with a little oil, grate a generous amount of Parmesan over and finish with a few turns of the peppermill.

warm roquefort tarts with red onion jam

Use frozen puff pastry for these tarts, for which you will need four individual 4-inch tart pans with removable bases. The amounts can be doubled for eight. The onion relish is enough for eight servings, but it is good with cheese or terrines and keeps in the refrigerator for at least a week.

Instead of Roquefort, you could use any other strongly flavored blue cheese, such as Gippsland or Gorgonzola. You could further ring the changes by substituting a crisp shortcrust or even phyllo pastry for the puff. If using phyllo, use six buttered sheets one on top of the other.

8 ounces puff pastry
1 egg
6 ounces Roquefort or
  other blue cheese, crumbled
¼ cup mascarpone cheese

for the red onion jam:
2 pounds red onions, thinly
  sliced
⅔ cup olive oil
2 teaspoons superfine sugar
salt and pepper

serves 4

First make the red onion jam: put the onions in a heavy casserole with the oil, set over a low heat and cook for 30 minutes, stirring from time to time. Turn up the heat to medium, sprinkle on the sugar and season with salt and pepper. Continue to cook, stirring continuously, until caramelized, and set aside.

Roll out the pastry to a thickness of about ¼ inch and use to line the 4 tart pans (see above). Put these into the freezer to chill. Preheat the oven to 400°F.

In a bowl, beat the egg lightly, then add the blue cheese and the mascarpone. Beat to a stiff paste. Spoon this into the tartlet shells.

Bake for 20 minutes, until the tops are a golden bubbling brown.

Remove from the pan, transfer to individual plates and put a neat spoon of the onion jam beside each tart.

baked polenta with blue cheese and braised broad beans

Serve this dish at room temperature with some good crusty bread. Italian delicatessens, small specialty-food stores and — these days — even some supermarkets, are good sources for artisanal loaves.

scant 1 cup milk
⅔ cup light cream or
   half-and-half
1 garlic clove
salt and pepper
½ cup instant polenta
4½ ounces Gorgonzola
   dolcelatte or Gippsland blue
   cheese

for the braised fava beans:
5 tablespoons olive oil
2 garlic cloves, finely chopped
2 fresh thyme sprigs
¾ cup shelled fava beans
salt and pepper
1 tablespoon chopped fresh
   flat-leaf parsley

serves 4

In a heavy-bottomed saucepan, bring 1 cup water, the milk and 7 tablespoons of the cream to a boil. Add the garlic and 1 teaspoon each salt and pepper, then turn down the heat to produce a rolling simmer. Add the polenta and whisk it in. Cook for 40 to 50 minutes over low heat, whisking vigorously every 5 minutes to prevent it from sticking.

Whisk in the cheese and remaining cream — making sure the cheese is evenly distributed — and cook for a final 5 minutes. Then pour onto a large flat plate and leave to cool to room temperature.

To braise the fava beans, pour the olive oil into a saucepan over low heat. When the oil becomes aromatic, add the garlic and thyme, stir and allow to infuse for 1 to 2 minutes. Add the fava beans and season with ½ teaspoon of salt and a few turns of pepper. With the heat at its lowest setting, simmer gently for 15 minutes. Remove from the heat and stir in the parsley. Leave to cool at room temperature.

When both the polenta and the beans are at room temperature, slice the polenta into ½-inch-thick fingers. Put 2 or 3 of these on each of 4 plates. Spoon over the beans and oil, and finish with a few turns of the peppermill.

penne with fennel, fresh peas and olive oil

Fresh peas are a seasonal pleasure that too many people ignore after years of frozen petit peas, although, of course, these can still be used to good effect. A delicious alternative in this recipe is to substitute the first tiny fava beans of summer before they have formed a skin. When cooking dried pastas there are no absolute cooking times, since these vary from manufacturer to manufacturer, so use the packet instructions as a rough guideline, but start testing the pasta regularly near the estimated time and drain as soon as the pasta is just al dente.

salt
1 or 2 fennel bulbs, 14 ounces
  total weight
1 large leek, about 3½ ounces,
  white part only
⅔ cup olive oil
pepper
¾ cup shelled peas
14 ounces penne
freshly grated Parmesan
  cheese, to serve

serves 4

In a large pan, 4 quarts of water to a boil with about 1 tablespoon salt.

Cut off the feathery tops from the fennel bulb(s) and reserve. Cut the bulb(s) into ½-inch cubes. Cut the leek lengthwise in half and then in half again. Chop it finely.

Put the olive oil in a pan over medium heat and when the oil is aromatic, add the fennel and leek. Season with salt and pepper. Gently cook this mixture, stirring for 2 minutes, then add ⅔ cup of water. Bring slowly to a boil, put on the lid and simmer gently for 20 minutes.

Coarsely chop the fennel tops and add to the pan with the peas. Cook for a further 10 minutes with the lid off. Taste and season as necessary.

Using the packet instructions as a rough guideline, calculate when to put the penne in to cook so that the pasta and sauce are ready at the same time. Drain the penne in a colander, allowing the water to drain completely, and transfer to a large warmed bowl. Add the fennel and pea sauce and toss to mix.

Transfer to a warmed serving dish and serve immediately, with a bowl of Parmesan on the table.

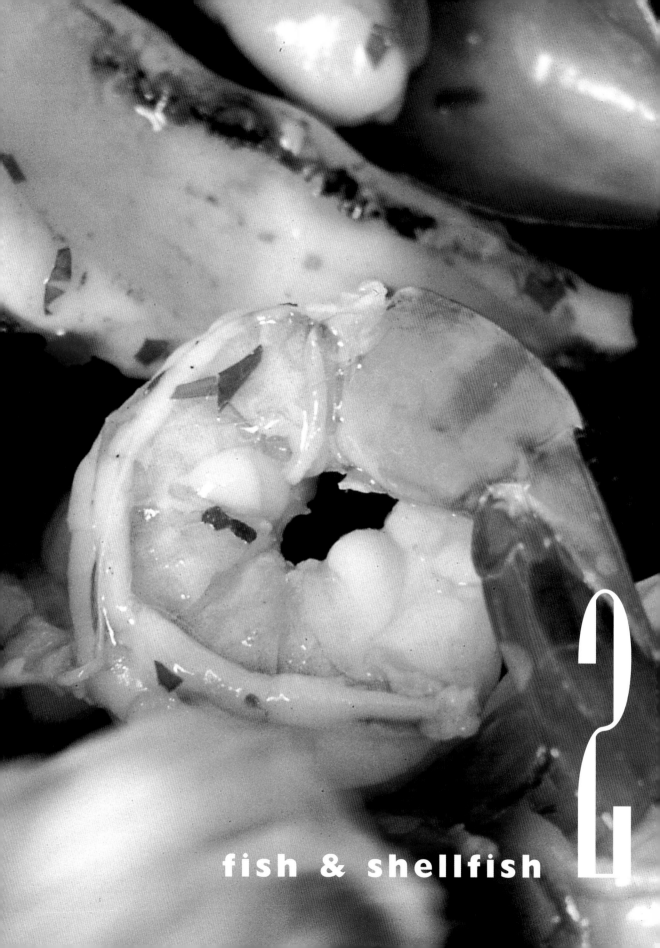

fish & shellfish

2

snapper steamed with parsley, white wine and olive oil

This gentle treatment makes a simple but delicious summer dish that is equally appropriate for sea bass fillets. Serve with a salad of iceberg lettuce, ripe plum tomatoes, flat-leaf parsley and Ligurian olives.

2 tablespoons dry white wine
5 tablespoons extra-virgin
  olive oil
I garlic clove, finely chopped
2 tablespoons chopped fresh
  flat-leaf parsley
salt and pepper
4 skinless snapper fillets, each
  about 6 ounces

serves 4

Have ready a large flat-bottomed frying pan and cut a sheet of parchment paper so that it will fit snugly inside the rim of the pan.

Pour the wine, olive oil and $1/4$ cup water into the empty pan. Add the garlic, parsley and a teaspoon of salt and $1/2$ teaspoon of pepper. Bring to a boil, lower the heat to a simmer and lay the fillets close together in the center of the pan. Put the parchment paper over the pan, tucking it down around the edges to touch the poaching liquid. Cover and steam for 6 to 7 minutes until just done, when the flesh will be opaque and firm to the touch.

Remove the fish with a slotted spatula and transfer to warmed serving plates. Spoon over some of the cooking liquid as a sauce.

panfried john dory with garlic butter and fennel

The John Dory are cooked whole for individual serving, so you don't want fish larger than $1 1/8$ pounds. Slightly smaller is desirable; otherwise by the time it is cooked around the bone the flesh nearer the skin will be overdone. You will need to use two frying pans to cook this number of fish in one go. The garlic is cooked very gently in a mixture of butter and olive oil until sweet and tender, bringing out all the flavor without making it bitter. Serve with creamy mashed potatoes (page 69). If you can't get John Dory, porgy and flounder both respond well to this treatment.

6 tablespoons butter
$1/2$ cup olive oil
4 large garlic cloves, sliced
  wafer-thin

Over low heat, put one-third of the butter and half the oil in each of 2 frying pans. Put half the garlic slices and half the chili shreds into each pan. Cook gently, stirring from time to time, for 10 minutes. Remove the fried garlic and chili with a slotted spoon and reserve.

fish & shellfish

1 small green chili, seeded and
  shredded
4 whole John Dory, each
  weighing about 1 pound,
  cleaned
¼ cup all-purpose flour
¾ cup finely chopped
  fennel fronds
salt and pepper

serves 4

Rinse the fish under cold running water, then pat dry with paper
towels. Season well with salt and pepper and dust with the flour.

Turn the heat up to full under the pans and, after 30 seconds, add 2
fish to each pan. Fry for 1 minute on each side to brown the skin, then
turn the heat down to medium and cook for a further 2 minutes on
each side. Carefully transfer the fish to a warmed serving plate.

Return the garlic and chili to one of the pans with the remaining
butter. Add the fennel and stir over medium heat for a minute. Spoon
this sauce over the fish and serve at once.

roast salmon with vermouth and spinach

4 pieces salmon fillet with skin
  intact, each about 8 ounces,
  scaled
1 shallot, finely chopped
3 tablespoons Noilly Prat
  dry white vermouth
2 tablespoons white wine
  vinegar
2 tablespoons heavy cream
¾ cup butter
salt and pepper
2 tablespoons olive oil
14 ounces spinach

serves 4

Preheat an oven to 475°F. Feel carefully along the salmon for any
small pin bones and remove them.

Put the shallot into a small saucepan with the vermouth and vinegar
and bring to a boil. Reduce down to 1 teaspoon of liquid, then add in
the cream. Allow this to boil, then turn down the heat to a simmer
and, whisking all the time, gradually add all but 1 tablespoon of the
butter, diced small, until fully incorporated. Season with salt and
pepper, pass through a fine sieve into a warm bowl and reserve in a
warm place.

Select a heavy ovenproof frying pan that is large enough to hold the
salmon pieces in one layer not touching. Put this over high heat and
season the fish all over. When the pan is very hot, add the oil, turning
and tilting it quickly to coat the surface. Lay the salmon in the pan, skin
side down, and leave for 1 to 2 minutes, then transfer to the oven and
roast for 7 to 8 minutes. Remove and set side.

In a wok or large frying pan over high heat, melt the remaining butter
and start to add the spinach leaves, a handful at a time, adding more
as they wilt. Season, empty into a colander and drain.

Working quickly, put the spinach in a bowl then, using tongs, divide it
among 4 warmed plates, mounding it in the center. Spoon the sauce
around and use a spatula to place the salmon on top, crisp skin
upward. Serve at once.

crispy fried turmeric fish with balinese chili sambal

The wok lends itself to frying whole fish or large pieces of fish on the bone, a technique widely used throughout Southeast Asia and which achieves a crisp finish using only a limited amount of oil. The size of the fish is critical: more than 1½ pounds and you have a problem, both in cooking the fish to the desired depth without overcooking the outer flesh and in turning it without breaking it. Here the required weight is only 12 ounces per fish, the perfect size when cut into two pieces. Have the fishmonger clean, scale and gut the fish for you.

When it is necessary to rub turmeric into something by hand, you may prefer to wear rubber gloves to avoid turning out next day with oddly yellow fingers.

A pleasing accompaniment to fried fish is a Balinese chili sambal with some fresh Vietnamese mint or Thai basil stirred into it. Sambals are strongly flavored relishes that are omnipresent in both Indonesia and Malaysia. The traditional method of preparation is with a pestle and mortar, while the food processor makes it effortless.

2 whole porgies, each weighing about 12 ounces
1 teaspoon ground turmeric
1½ teaspoons salt
½ cup sunflower oil
2 small limes

for the Balinese chili sambal:
4 large paprika peppers or large mild red chilies
6 large hot red chilies
4 garlic cloves, coarsely chopped
1 teaspoon shrimp paste (see page 156)
6 tablespoons sunflower oil
8 fresh Thai basil leaves, shredded
1 teaspoon salt

serves 4

First make the sambal (this can be made days in advance and kept in a jar in the refrigerator; since it goes well with many dishes, you can make double or treble this amount): seed the peppers and chilies. Put them in a food processor with the garlic and pulse-chop to a coarse-textured paste. Don't take it too far or it will separate and become watery. Put the oil in a wok or deep-sided frying pan and place over medium-high heat. When hot, fry the chili paste with the shrimp paste, stirring frequently and not allowing it to stick, for 3 to 4 minutes. Remove from the heat.

Score the fish on both sides with a series of shallow cuts to help the heat penetrate the flesh, then cut each fish in half lengthwise to give 4 equal pieces. Mix the turmeric and salt together then rub this uniformly into the fish and leave at room temperature for 1 hour.

Pour the oil into a wok or deep-sided frying pan over medium heat. When very hot, which takes a minute or two, lay the fish in and cook for 5 to 6 minutes each side. The aim is a crisp golden exterior. Remove with a slotted spatula or slotted spoon and drain on paper towels for 30 seconds, then transfer to a warmed serving dish.

To serve, cut the limes in half and arrange around the fish. Stir the basil into the sambal, season with the salt and serve it separately.

5 tablespoons sunflower oil

4 garlic cloves, chopped

1 red chili, halved lengthwise
  and seeded, then cut
  into julienne strips

3 tablespoons finely chopped
  cilantro leaves, plus 2
  tablespoons finely chopped
  cilantro roots

3½ tablespoons fish stock

1 tablespoon fish sauce

serves 4

to a boil, lower the heat and simmer until the peas are just tender, about 30 minutes. Strain through a sieve, reserving 4 tablespoons of the cooking liquid. Chop all but 3 tablespoons of the split peas.

Put a wok over high heat and when hot, swirl in 3 tablespoons of the oil. As it begins to shimmer, throw in the chopped ginger, garlic, chili and chopped cilantro roots. Stir-fry for 30 seconds, then stir in the chopped peas. Add the whole split peas, the reserved cooking liquid and the fish stock. Cook, stirring, for 30 seconds. Remove from the heat, scrape into a bowl and reserve.

Wipe out the wok, add the remaining oil and when hot, put in the fish and brown, tossing. Add the reserved split pea sauce with the remaining ginger, lower the heat and simmer for 4 minutes. Carefully stir in the fish sauce and scatter over the cilantro leaves.

Serve with jasmine rice (page 154).

red shrimp and pea eggplant curry

When pea eggplants are unobtainable, substitute small, slender Asian eggplants, but cut them into grape-sized pieces and add them to the sauce 3 to 4 minutes before the shrimp.

2½ cups canned coconut milk

4 tablespoons red curry paste
  (page 155)

1⅛ pounds fresh raw shrimp,
  peeled and deveined

12 pea eggplants, stems removed

2 kaffir lime leaves, shredded

1 cup fresh cilantro leaves,
  shredded

1 cup fresh Thai basil leaves,
  shredded

serves 4

Pour three-quarters of the coconut milk into a wok or deep-frying pan and bring to a boil. Stir in the curry paste. Boil rapidly to reduce and, when the mixture starts to thicken and become oily, add the remaining milk. Bring back to a boil and add the shrimp followed by the eggplant. Cook for 1 to 2 minutes.

Scatter over the shredded lime leaves, basil and cilantro, and serve immediately with jasmine rice (page 154).

seafood salad with chili dressing

With the exception of the mussels, all the seafood is cooked on a stove-top pan. It is up to you what mixture of salad leaves you use, but it should be a combination of bitter, peppery and sweet. For example, radicchio, watercress and oakleaf lettuce would work, or arugula, Belgian endive and mâche. If time is pressing, buy one of those bags of ready-washed mixed leaves at the supermarket.

12 tiger prawns, thawed if frozen

4 scallops

1 pound cleaned squid

1 pound snapper fillets,
  skinned and cut into
  bite-sized pieces

4 tablespoons olive oil

salt and pepper

20 mussels

⅔ cup dry white wine

handful of flat-leaf fresh parsley

2 celery stalks, chopped

1 kaffir lime leaf

1 small hot red chili, cut into
  tiny dice

1 shallot, cut into tiny dice

5 tablespoons extra-virgin
  olive oil

juice of 1 lime

8 ounces mixed salad leaves
  (see above)

Peel the prawns, reserving the shells. Devein them, then cut down almost all the way through the flesh and press gently to "butterfly" them open. Put them into heavily salted ice water and rub them between your fingers for 2 minutes. Drain and rinse them. (This "sweetening" process improves the flavor of frozen shellfish.) Cut the scallops into 2 or 3 disks, depending on size. Cut a neat diamond crosshatch into the outside surface of each squid tube and cut the tentacles into 4 clumps.

Put the prepared prawns, scallops, squid and the pieces of snapper into a bowl with the olive oil and salt and pepper and toss to coat.

Scrub and debeard the mussels, discarding any that do not close when tapped. Put the wine into a saucepan in which the mussels will sit in a single layer, add them and bring to a boil. Shake the pan, put on the lid and cook over high heat, shaking from time to time, for about 2 minutes until most of the mussels have opened. Strain through a sieve into another pan, discarding any which have not opened. To the strained cooking liquid, add the prawn shells and heads, stems from the parsley sprigs, celery and lime leaf. Bring to a boil, lower the heat and simmer for 20 minutes. You want to have about 2 to 3 tablespoons of intensely flavored reduction left. If there is more, turn up the heat and reduce to the required amount. Strain through a sieve into a large bowl.

While this is reducing, open the mussels, leaving them on the half shell.

Add the chili and shallot to the reduction together with half the extra-virgin olive oil and the lime juice. Taste and season with salt and pepper. Add the mussels and toss them.

Put the salad leaves in a bowl and dress them lightly with the remaining olive oil and a few drops of balsamic vinegar. Season only with pepper and toss to coat.

fish & shellfish

**few drops of balsamic
    vinegar**

serves 6

Put a ridged grill pan on to heat until smoking hot. Cook the prawns, scallops, squid and snapper chunks briefly on it, turning each piece once. The different elements will cook at different speeds, but should only just be opaque in the middle. While still hot, add them to the dressing with the mussels and toss to coat.

Arrange the salad leaves on plates and distribute the seafood on top. , Scatter over the whole parsley leaves and serve while the seafood is still warm.

warm lobster salad with tomato confit and braised jerusalem artichokes

2 lobsters, each about
  1 1/2 pounds
4 braised Jerusalem artichokes in
  olive oil (page 116), drained and
  thinly sliced
1 small frisée lettuce,
  separated
1 tablespoon whole fresh chervil
  leaves

for the tomato confit:
1 1/8 pounds (about 6)
  ripe plum tomatoes
1/2 teaspoon finely chopped
  fresh rosemary
1/2 teaspoon finely chopped
  fresh thyme
1/2 teaspoon finely chopped
  fresh oregano
2 garlic cloves, thinly sliced
salt and pepper
about 2/3 cup extra-virgin olive oil

serves 4

Several days ahead, make the confit: preheat an oven to 230°F. Blanch the tomatoes briefly in boiling water, then peel them and cut into quarters. Seed them and lay the tomato pieces, not touching, on a baking sheet. Sprinkle over the herbs and garlic, ensuring that each piece is flavored with all of them. Scatter 1/4 teaspoon of salt and some coarsely ground pepper over all. Drizzle with 1 tablespoon of oil and put the baking sheet in the cool oven for 2 1/2 hours. This slow drying intensifies the flavor. Remove from the oven and allow to cool, then transfer to a sterilized jar and cover with extra-virgin olive oil. Keep refrigerated.

On the day of serving: put a large pot of water to boil over the highest heat, adding 2 heaped tablespoons of salt per quart.

Add the lobsters to the pot when the water is boiling furiously. Cook for 13 to 14 minutes and remove. Leave until they are cool enough to handle, then cut in half with a large knife, placing them belly side down and slitting them through the center from head to tail. Discard the intestinal tract and pull out the tail meat with a fork (it lifts out easily in one piece). Crack the claws with the back of a heavy knife to remove the flesh, pulling the blade bone away with the pincer and discard. You now have 6 pieces of meat. Cut them into 1-inch chunks.

Put the lobster in a large bowl together with the drained pieces of tomato confit and the sliced Jerusalem artichokes, followed by the frisée leaves, chervil and 2 tablespoons of olive oil from the confit jar. Season with pepper and toss to coat, then mound on 4 plates to serve while the lobster is still warm, milling a little more pepper over before bringing to the table.

seared scallops with squid-ink pasta and mascarpone

You can make your own pasta for this dish, as described on page 152, but any packaged squid-ink pasta is fine as long as it is a thin noodle like spaghetti or linguine. If using ready-made pasta, whether fresh or dry, use the package instructions as a rough guide and cook until just al dente. For homemade, allow 2 to 3 minutes from the water returning to a rapid boil.

7 ounces mascarpone cheese
¹/₄ cup grated Parmesan cheese
salt and pepper
20 plump scallops
2 tablespoons olive oil
7 ounces squid-ink pasta
  (page 152)
²/₃ cup finely chopped
  fresh chives

serves 4

Melt the mascarpone in a saucepan over low heat. When hot, add the grated Parmesan. Season with pepper, stir in and remove from the heat.

In another large pan, add ½ tablespoon of salt to about 2½ quarts of water and bring to a boil.

Season the scallops with salt and pepper and put a heavy frying pan over high heat. When it is hot, add 1 tablespoon of the olive oil and quickly turn and tilt the pan to coat the base. Add the scallops, searing and coloring the first surface for 2 minutes, then turning with tongs. At this point, put the pasta into the rapidly boiling water to cook (you will probably need to start this process earlier if using dried pasta). Give the scallops 2 minutes on the other side and transfer to a warm plate.

Work as quickly as possible during this final phase. As soon as the pasta is cooked, drain well in a colander and transfer to a large warmed bowl. Add the remaining oil, toss and season with pepper.

Wind one-quarter of the pasta around a fork into the shape of a ball and put this in the center of a warmed plate; repeat with the remaining pasta. Surround the balls of pasta with the seared scallops. Use a spoon to drizzle the mascarpone sauce over the scallops. Sprinkle with the chives and serve at once.

3

meat &
poultry

braised short-cut ribs of beef with lima beans and parsley

This uniquely Australian cut, which takes the meat with the upper section of the ribs so that it looks rather like a bandoleer of cartridges, is perfect for braising or stewing. You could ask your butcher to prepare it for you. If you can't get lima beans, serve the ribs with Creamy Mashed Potatoes (page 69).

2 ounces fresh flat-leaf
  parsley sprigs
1 ounce fresh thyme sprigs
3 bay leaves
1 pig's foot or ½ calf's
  foot
4 cups robust red wine
3½ pounds short-cut ribs
  of beef (see above)
2 tablespoons all-purpose flour
2 tablespoons vegetable oil
2 large carrots, cut into 4 pieces
2 celery stalks, cut into 4 pieces
1 large onion, cut into 4 pieces
1 leek, cut into 4 pieces
3 garlic cloves
4½ cups beef stock (page 152)
¼ teaspoon peppercorns
1½ tablespoons unsalted butter

for the lima beans and parsley:
1 cup dried lima beans, soaked
  overnight
3 tablespoons olive oil
2 garlic cloves, finely chopped
2 tablespoon chopped fresh
  flat-leaf parsley
2 tablespoons unsalted butter
salt and pepper

serves 4

Well ahead of time, cook the beef: tie the parsley, thyme and bay leaves in a bundle with string. Blanch the foot in boiling water, drain and rinse. Reserve. Pour the wine into a large saucepan over high heat and reduce by half.

At the same time, put a large frying pan over medium heat. Roll the beef in seasoned flour. Put 1 tablespoon of the oil in the pan and brown the ribs in 2 batches, turning until well caramelized. Wipe out the pan between batches, adding fresh oil. When browned, transfer the meat to the pan of reduced wine. Add the foot, the vegetables, garlic, herbs and ¼ teaspoon black peppercorns, then pour the stock over. Bring to a boil, skim and lower the heat to a bare simmer for 1¼ hours. Turn off the heat and leave to cool.

While the beef is cooling, prepare the beans: drain and wash them, then place them in a saucepan and cover with water. Bring to a boil, turn down the heat, and simmer for 25 to 30 minutes, or until tender. Remove from the heat and reserve.

Choose a heavy-based saucepan about the same size as the one in which you cooked the beans, pour in the olive oil and put over low heat. Stir in the garlic and cook for 1 minute, then stir in the parsley. Drain the beans and add them to the pan, stirring to coat. Add the butter and season with salt and pepper. As soon as the beans are glazed and piping hot, transfer to a warmed serving bowl.

When the beef is cool, transfer it to a bowl and cover with plastic wrap. Pass the cooking liquid through a fine sieve into a clean saucepan, discarding the foot, vegetables and bouquet garni. Bring to a boil and reduce to 1¼ cups.

Add the beef to this reduction with the butter and simmer for 2 to 3 minutes to warm through. Serve in large, warmed soup plates with the lima beans.

corned beef with horseradish dumplings

Corned beef, sometimes called salted silverside, is universally available in butchers' shops and supermarkets both in Australia and the United States.

piece of corned beef, 2½ pounds
2 large carrots, halved
1 large onion
1 leek, halved lengthwise
3 celery stalks, halved
  lengthwise
2 bay leaves
¼ teaspoon peppercorns
handful of parsley stems
Dijon mustard, to serve

for the horseradish dumplings:
1½ cups self-rising flour
fresh white bread crumbs
4 teaspoons grated horseradish
1 tablespoon chopped
  fresh parsley
6 tablespoons butter,
  cut into ½-inch dice
1 egg white

serves 4

Put the meat in a large pan and cover with water. Bring to a boil and skim any scum that comes to the surface. Add the vegetables, turn down to a medium simmer and add the bay leaves, peppercorns and parsley stems. Cook for 1 hour 40 minutes, topping up with water as necessary to keep the meat covered.

About 25 minutes before the end of cooking time, make the dumplings: put the flour, bread crumbs, grated horseradish, chopped parsley, and butter in a food processor. Blitz to a crumb texture. With the machine still running, add the egg white through the feeder tube. Then add in a little cold water, just enough so the dough balls. With floured hands and on a floured surface, shape the dough into balls the size of Ping-Pong balls. Poach in simmering salted water for about 20 minutes, when they should be well risen and light. Remove with a slotted spoon.

When the beef is cooked, with a slotted spoon, transfer the cooked vegetables in the beef pot to a warmed serving plate. Carve the beef in ¼-inch slices, arrange them on the serving plate with the vegetables and dumplings and spoon over a little of the cooking liquid. Offer the mustard in a small bowl.

roast rack of lamb with beet confit

2 racks of lamb, each about
  12 ounces, back fat removed
2 tablespoons olive oil
4 fresh rosemary sprigs
4 garlic cloves, bruised
salt and pepper

for the beet confit:
1¼ pounds beet
½ cup red currant jelly
7 tablespoons red wine
4 tablespoons cider vinegar
salt and pepper

serves 4

First make the confit: in a heavy-bottomed saucepan over medium heat, melt the red currant jelly. On the coarsest plate of a grater, grate the beet into strips. Add these to the melted jelly and cook until they take on a glazed appearance. Add the red wine, then the vinegar and turn down the heat to a bare simmer. Reduce the mixture, stirring frequently, for about 30 minutes. Season with 1 teaspoon of salt and ¼ teaspoon of pepper before removing from the heat.

Halfway through reducing the confit, preheat the oven to 475°F. Put a roasting pan over medium heat. Add the oil and, when hot, sear the lamb on all sides. Add the rosemary and garlic, and season the racks well with salt and pepper. Put to roast for 12 to 15 minutes for a pink finish, 20 minutes for well done. Remove when done to your liking and leave to rest for 5 to 10 minutes. While the meat is resting, reheat the confit.

Carve the racks into chops, placing 3 on each warmed plate with a spoonful of the confit.

roast rack of lamb with chinese spices

1 teaspoon coarsely ground
  Sichuan pepper
2 teaspoons Asian sesame oil
1 cup maltose (page 157)
1-inch piece fresh ginger, peeled
  and chopped
1 garlic clove, chopped
3 or 4 star anise
1 teaspoon five-spice powder
2 racks of lamb, each about 12
  ounces, back fat removed

serves 4

The day before: in a small frying pan over low heat, dry-roast the Sichuan pepper until it starts to color. Remove and leave to cool, then grind coarsely through a pepper mill.

Put the maltose container in a saucepan of simmering water to liquefy the maltose, as you would for honey. Pour it into a large bowl with all the ingredients except the lamb; mix well. Let cool, then rub this glaze over the lamb. Put the lamb in a roasting pan, pour over the remaining glaze, and refrigerate overnight.

When ready to cook: preheat an oven to 425°F. Put a wire rack in a roasting pan and sit the lamb racks on this, bones upward. Roast for 12 to 15 minutes. Don't turn or baste during cooking. Remove and allow to rest for 10 minutes before carving. Serve with steamed bok choy, Chinese broccoli or spinach, or even a simple crisp green salad.

roast rack of new-season's lamb with beetroot confit

neck of lamb casserole with red onions, parsley and cilantro

Originally a stew of this sort would have been made from mutton, but neck of lamb has just the right proportion of meat to bone to give marvelous flavor and produce a rich yet simple broth. Using lots of herbs gives the dish an unexpected finish that is forceful without being overpowering. It could also be made with young goat.

2¼ pounds neck of lamb
5 tablespoons olive oil
2½ pounds potatoes, peeled and
  thinly sliced
1 pound red onions, thinly sliced
½ cup wild rice
1 large bunch fresh flat-leaf
  parsley, chopped
1 large bunch fresh
  cilantro, chopped
2 kaffir lime leaves
salt and pepper
1 teaspoon red pepper flakes
2 carrots, thinly sliced
5 cups chicken stock (page 153)

serves 6

Preheat an oven to 350°F. Trim off the skin and most of the fat from the lamb. Brush a dutch oven with some of the olive oil and put in a layer of one-third of the sliced potatoes. Put a layer of all the onions on that and scatter over half the wild rice, 5 tablespoons of the chopped parsley, 4 tablespoons of the chopped cilantro, and 1 of the lime leaves; and season with salt and pepper. Follow this with a layer of lamb. Scatter that with the chilies, then another layer of potato and all of the sliced carrots, the remaining wild rice, the second lime leaf and any remaining parsley and cilantro (reserving some whole leaves for garnish). Season again and finish with a layer of potato slices, neatly overlapping. Pour over the stock, adding water if necessary to bring the liquid level up to that of the top layer of potatoes. Brush the potato surface with the remaining olive oil.

Cover with a lid and bake in the oven for about 2 hours. Remove the lid and continue cooking for a further 20 to 30 minutes to brown and crisp the potatoes.

Serve in large bowls from the casserole at the table, scattering over the reserved whole leaves of parsley and cilantro.

meatballs and fettuccine with cilantro

The meatball is a universally traditional solution to making less tender cuts succulent, the ground meat being easily bound with moistening and flavoring agents to enhance its good points while minimizing any inherent defects. Here lamb neck fillet is trimmed of fat and then minced, before being blitzed in a food processor with seasoning. You can, of course, use ready-ground lamb, in which case buy the best lean mix with a 10 to 15 percent fat content. The resulting ground meat holds together tenaciously and when formed into balls, may be stuffed with this fresh-tasting aromatic pesto, or if preferred, a classic basil-and-pine-nut pesto.

1¼ pound lean ground lamb
1 teaspoon red pepper flakes
1 garlic clove, finely chopped
1 small bunch fresh chives
salt and pepper
1 quantity homemade pasta
   (page 151), or 12 ounces
   ready-made dried fettuccine
4 tablespoons olive oil

for the cilantro and pistachio pesto:
⅓ cup unsalted pistachio nuts
⅞ cup sunflower oil
1-inch piece fresh ginger, peeled
4 garlic cloves
1 hot green chili
1 bunch fresh cilantro,
   about 3 ounces
1 bunch fresh Thai basil,
   about 2 ounces
juice of ½ lemon

serves 4

First make the pesto: grind the nuts in a food processor. Heat 3 to 4 tablespoons of the oil in a frying pan and cook the ground nuts gently over low heat for about 5 minutes, stirring frequently. Leave to cool. Chop the ginger, garlic and chili. Put these in the processor with the nuts and the oil from the pan. Purée to a smooth, stiff paste. Chop the cilantro and basil and stir them in with the lemon juice. Season to taste.

If grinding the lamb yourself, trim off all visible fat before putting it through the finest grinding plate. Transfer to a food processor together with the chili flakes, the garlic, half the chives, finely chopped, and salt and pepper. Pulse-chop to combine, then work at full speed until the meat forms a paste. Fry a small piece and eat it to check the seasoning. Adjust the seasoning. Divide it into 16 balls. Push an opening into the middle with your finger and, with a small spoon, put a little of the pesto into it, forming the meat around to seal it in. Dust a baking sheet with flour and put them on this, then dust the tops also. The finished meatballs can be used immediately or wrapped in plastic wrap and kept for 2 hours in the refrigerator.

Finish the pesto sauce: with the food processor running, add the remaining oil in a thin, steady stream through the feed tube until you have a rich, smooth sauce. Put a large pan of salted water to boil.

Fry the meatballs gently in the olive oil over medium-low heat, rolling them to brown evenly. They take about 6 to 8 minutes.

At the same time, cook the pasta in rapidly boiling salted water for 3 minutes if homemade or using package instructions as a rough guide, until just al dente. Drain quickly in a colander, and return the pasta to the hot dry pan, while there is still a little water clinging to the pasta. Immediately add 4 to 6 tablespoons of the pesto and toss.

Mound the pasta in 4 warmed bowls, put the meatballs on top and scatter over the remaining chives snipped into ½-inch pieces.

braised spiced lamb shanks with lemon pickle and couscous

The preparation of this dish involves some planning, although the first stages are the lengthy ones and can be done well in advance. Finishing the dish then takes less than 30 minutes.

salt
1 teaspoon lemon juice
4 lamb shanks, each about
   14 ounces
⅓ cup dried chickpeas
1 small bunch fresh cilantro
3 carrots
1 celery stalk
1 onion
½ leek
3 garlic cloves
2-inch piece of fresh ginger
3 tablespoons vegetable oil
3 star anise
4½ cups beef stock (page 152)
1¾ cups dry white wine
lemon pickle (page 150)

for the spicy marinade:
1 bunch fresh cilantro,
   including roots
3 garlic cloves, finely chopped
2-inch piece of fresh ginger,
   very finely chopped
1 teaspoon pepper
1 teaspoon ground ginger
½ teaspoon ground turmeric
½ teaspoon saffron threads
5 tablespoons thick yogurt

for the couscous:
½ teaspoon salt
1 tablespoon sunflower oil
1½ cups couscous
1 tablespoon butter, melted

serves 4

The day before: rub 1 teaspoon of salt and the lemon juice into the lamb shanks and leave to marinate for 2 to 3 hours.

Prepare the spicy marinade: peel the cilantro roots and wash them, then chop with the stems and leaves. Put all into a large bowl with the garlic and ginger, then add the dry spices followed by the yogurt. Mix all together, add the lamb shanks and turn to coat. Leave to marinate overnight in the refrigerator. Put the chickpeas to soak in cold water overnight.

When ready to cook: preheat the oven to 400°F.

Prepare the braising vegetables: pick the leaves from the cilantro sprigs and reserve them for the garnish. Coarsely chop 1 of the carrots, the celery, onion, leek, garlic and ginger. Remove the shanks from the marinade and wipe them dry.

Put a large heavy frying pan over medium-high heat and add half the oil. When hot, brown the shanks all over, then transfer them to a deep dutch oven. Brown the braising vegetables in the remaining oil and add to the shanks with the star anise. Pour over the stock and wine and bring to a boil. Cover and braise in the oven for 2 hours, when the meat will be tender. Remove and leave to cool.

While the lamb is braising, prepare the garnish by boiling the chickpeas in lightly salted water for 25 minutes and, separately, the remaining carrots cut into 1-inch pieces in salted water until just tender. Leave both to cool in their cooking water.

Remove the shanks from the braising liquid and transfer to a plate while you make the sauce. Sieve the braising liquid into a saucepan and reduce over a high heat to about ⅔ cup.

After the sauce has been reducing for 10 to 12 minutes, prepare the couscous: in another pan add the salt to 1½ cups water and bring to a boil. Add the oil, then pour in the couscous and turn off the heat.

66

Leave to absorb the water for 4 to 5 minutes, then add the butter and gently stir with a fork to separate the grains.

Just before you add the couscous to the water, add the shanks to the reduced sauce with the carrots, chickpeas and cilantro leaves and warm through gently for 5 minutes.

To serve, put a lamb shank on each of 4 warmed plates and spoon the sauce and vegetables generously over it. Serve the couscous separately from a large bowl, offering the lemon pickle at the table.

cotechino, fresh bacon and beans

Cotechino is a boiling sausage made in the Emilia-Romagna region of Italy and a particular specialty of Modena, where it is traditionally served hot with lentils, although it is equally good with beans or polenta. It gets its name from *cotica*, the Italian word for "pork rind," which is a principal ingredient of the sausage and gives it its characteristic gelatinous quality.

1 piece fresh bacon, 2¼ pounds
⅔ cup salt
½ teaspoon crushed
   peppercorns
2 fresh thyme sprigs
2 bay leaves
1 cotechino sausage,
   10½ to 14 ounces
1 onion, halved
1 cinnamon stick

for the beans:
scant 1 cup cannellini beans,
   soaked overnight
5 tablespoons olive oil
3 garlic cloves, finely chopped
14 ounces ripe plum (Roma)
   tomatoes, peeled, seeded and
   quartered
3 fresh thyme sprigs
2 bay leaves
salt and pepper

serves 4

Two days ahead, salt the fresh bacon: mix the salt and peppercorns together then rub them into the bacon. Put it in a shallow pan, bruise the thyme and bay leaves and add to the pan. Cover with plastic wrap and refrigerate for 2 days, turning over the second day.

About 4 hours ahead on the day of serving: rinse the salted bacon under cold running water, then put it in a large pot with the cotechino, onion and the cinnamon stick. Cover with cold water and bring to a boil. Turn down the heat and simmer for 1 hour. Turn off the heat and leave to cool in the cooking liquid.

Prepare the beans: drain the soaked beans and wash them in cold water. Drain again and put into a saucepan with 3½ cups of the pork cooking liquid. Bring to a boil, skim, lower the heat and simmer for 30 minutes.

In a second large heavy-bottomed saucepan over medium heat, heat the olive oil. After a minute, add the garlic and cook this for a minute, then add the tomatoes, thyme and bay leaves. Turn down the heat and simmer for 10 minutes.

Drain the beans, reserving ½ cup of the cooking liquid, and add them both to the tomatoes. Continue to cook for another 30 minutes. Season with salt and pepper and remove from the heat.

Remove the cotechino from the liquid and reheat the bacon in the liquid. Cut the cotechino into 1-inch slices, add to the beans, stir in and reheat gently.

Remove the bacon and cut into ½-inch slices. Put 3 slices on each of 4 warmed plates, then 2 pieces of sausage and a large spoonful of beans. Serve at once, perhaps with a glass of light Italian red wine and some crusty bread.

pancetta-and-basil-wrapped chicken, mashed potatoes and gravy

Buy the pancetta for this dish thinly sliced to order from an Italian delicatessen. Since it is very salty you will not need any further salt to season the dish. The potatoes should also not be too buttery, as the sauce is very rich. Choose floury potatoes; in Australia, Toolangi Delight are a good choice, as are Golden Wonder and Red Pontiac anywhere else.

8 thin slices pancetta
½ cup fresh basil leaves
4 skinned chicken breast halves
pepper
2 tablespoons olive oil
2 tablespoons butter
2½ cups strongly flavored
  chicken stock (page 152)
7 tablespoons heavy cream
1 small bunch fresh chives

for the creamy mashed potatoes:
2½ pounds floury potatoes,
  peeled
generous 4 tablespoons butter, at
  room temperature
7 tablespoons milk, heated
salt and pepper

serves 4

Preheat an oven to 425°F. Put the potatoes in a large pan of salted water to boil.

Lay 2 slices of pancetta slightly overlapping on a work surface. Put one-quarter of the basil leaves on top, season with pepper and lay a chicken breast on top. Carefully roll the prosciutto over and wrap securely.

Put the olive oil and butter in a frying pan large enough to hold the 4 wrapped breasts in a single layer (or use 2 pans). Lay them in carefully and fry for 4 minutes on each side. Transfer to a roasting pan and put in the oven for 10 minutes.

As soon as they go in the oven, pour the stock into the pan and reduce by half over high heat, scraping any bits from the pan with a wooden spoon. Off the heat, whisk in the cream and all but 8 of the chive stalks, chopped. Taste and add more pepper if needed. Keep warm.

Drain the potatoes in a colander, leave for 1 minute to dry, then return to the pan and mash dry with a potato masher. Beat in the butter with a wooden spoon, then the milk. Taste and adjust the seasoning with salt and pepper. Transfer to a warmed serving bowl.

Put a wrapped chicken breast on each plate and spoon the cream gravy around it. Scatter over the remaining 8 chives snipped into 1-inch lengths. Offer the mashed potatoes at the table for people to help themselves.

chicken with a parmesan and herb crust

Boned and skinned chicken breasts can be treated like veal escalopes, emerging from their brief cooking perfectly moist and tender, the crisp crust a nice contrast to the moist interior. You can get your butcher to skin, bone and flatten the breasts for you; if buying from a supermarket, do it yourself.

4 chicken breast halves, skinned
 and boned
$^1/_2$ cup fresh white
 bread crumbs
$^3/_4$ cup grated Parmesan cheese
1 tablespoon chopped
 fresh basil
1 tablespoon chopped
 fresh oregano
1 tablespoon chopped
 fresh parsley
salt and pepper
1 egg
3$^1/_2$ tablespoons milk
2 tablespoons olive oil
4 tablespoons unsalted butter

serves 4

If preparing the chicken yourself, skin the breasts, trim off any residual fat or cartilage and put them, one at a time, between sheets of plastic wrap and, with a rolling pin, beat out gently into thin escalopes.

Put the bread crumbs, Parmesan and herbs in a bowl. Season with $^1/_2$ teaspoon salt and $^1/_4$ teaspoon pepper. Mix together well. In another bowl, whisk the egg, then whisk in the milk.

Pass each flattened breast through the egg mixture, allowing excess to drip back into the bowl, then press it into the coating mixture, first one side and then the other. Press down with the palm of your hand to ensure an even coating and transfer the breasts to a baking sheet, not touching (if they sit on top of one another they tend to go soggy).

Put 1 tablespoon of the oil in a large frying pan over medium heat. When hot, swirl in half the butter and, as it sizzles, carefully lay in 2 chicken pieces. Give them 2 to 3 minutes on each side. Keep warm in a low oven while you cook the others. Alternatively, use 2 pans and cook in tandem.

crisp fried chicken with chili and cilantro butter

Once upon a time there was chicken Kiev, a very popular dish but one served exclusively in restaurants, private cooks deeming it to be far too difficult to make at home. Your classic chicken Kiev is a skinned suprême, that is, the boneless breast attached to the scraped wing bone, with the pinion bone removed. To make Kiev, the fillet is removed from the middle of the suprême and the remaining flesh is then beaten into an escalope. The small fillet is opened and stuffed with a piece of chilled herbed butter. The escalope is wrapped around it and the whole is coated in egg and crumbs and then deep-fried. This is all more difficult to describe than it is to do. In this version, chili and cilantro butter is substituted for the usual *maître d'hôtel* (parsley) butter.

4 chicken suprêmes
salt and pepper
2 eggs, beaten
heaping 1 cup fine dried
  bread crumbs
1 lemon, quartered
  lengthwise to serve

for the chili and cilantro butter:
½ cup butter, at
  room temperature
½ cup finely chopped
  fresh cilantro
2 medium-hot green
  chilies, seeded and diced
salt and pepper

serves 4

First make the chili and cilantro butter: cream the butter in a bowl. Beat in the cilantro and chili with 1½ teaspoons of salt and ½ teaspoon of pepper. Scrape the mixture out on to a rectangle of foil, roll this up into a cylinder and chill to firm. It will keep in the refrigerator for a week or may be frozen for up to 2 months.

Remove the skin from each suprême and lay it skinned side down. Detach the small fillet and cut along its length and almost all the way through. Open it out and flatten it. Put one-quarter of the chilled chili butter in the middle and wrap it round it. Return these to the refrigerator. Open each breast in the same way, place it between sheets of plastic wrap and gently flatten it out with a meat pounder, rolling pin or child's wooden hammer until about ½ inch thick. Lay the small buttered fillet in the middle and wrap the escalope around it. Season with salt and pepper, then dip in beaten egg and then in bread crumbs. Repeat these coatings to give it a double crust. Repeat with remaining ingredients. Chill for at least 1 hour.

Preheat a deep-fryer or oil in a wok to 350°F and deep-fry the coated chicken for 7 to 8 minutes. When the crisp golden-brown shell is cut open the melted butter gushes out. Serve with French fries or creamy mashed potatoes (page 69) and with a lemon quarter.

roast chicken with tarragon, prosciutto and polenta

Let your butcher bone the chicken for you. When he or she can do preliminary work, freeing you to do more constructive things in the kitchen, why not? The specialist is always the best person from whom to buy anything — get your prosciutto from an Italian delicatessen, who will cut it fresh for you. As soon as you get it home, put it in a lock-top bag and refrigerate until needed. This is also the best way to buy and deal with salami or other cured sausages and meats like *lardo* or *bresaola*. Packets of pre-sliced meats are the worst possible choice, being both more expensive and, by definition, not freshly cut from the piece.

scant ¾ cup butter

3 tablespoons fresh tarragon
   leaves, chopped

salt and pepper

8 chicken thighs, boned and
   skinned

8 thin slices of prosciutto

1 quantity soft polenta
   (page 154)

1¾ cups strong chicken stock
   (page 152)

serves 4

Lightly cream the butter in a mixing bowl. Beat in the tarragon, 1 teaspoon of salt and ½ teaspoon coarsely ground pepper.

Place the chicken flat in front of you, open up the flaps where the bones have been removed and, using a small spoon, fill the cavity with the flavored butter. Fold the ends of the chicken into the center. Lay a slice of prosciutto on the work surface, put the stuffed chicken on top and wrap to enclose. Repeat and refrigerate for the butter to firm. This can be done several hours in advance.

Make the soft polenta (page 154); this takes about 50 minutes.

Preheat an oven to 475°F. Pour the stock into a deep roasting pan, place over medium heat and bring to a simmer. Place the chicken parcels in the stock, spacing them well apart, and cook in the oven for 20 to 25 minutes, basting from time to time. The prosciutto should be dark and crisp, but the center of the meat still moist.

Transfer the chicken to 4 warmed plates and put the pan over high heat. Reduce the stock rapidly by about half.

Place large spoonfuls of the polenta beside the chicken and spoon the sauce over and around it.

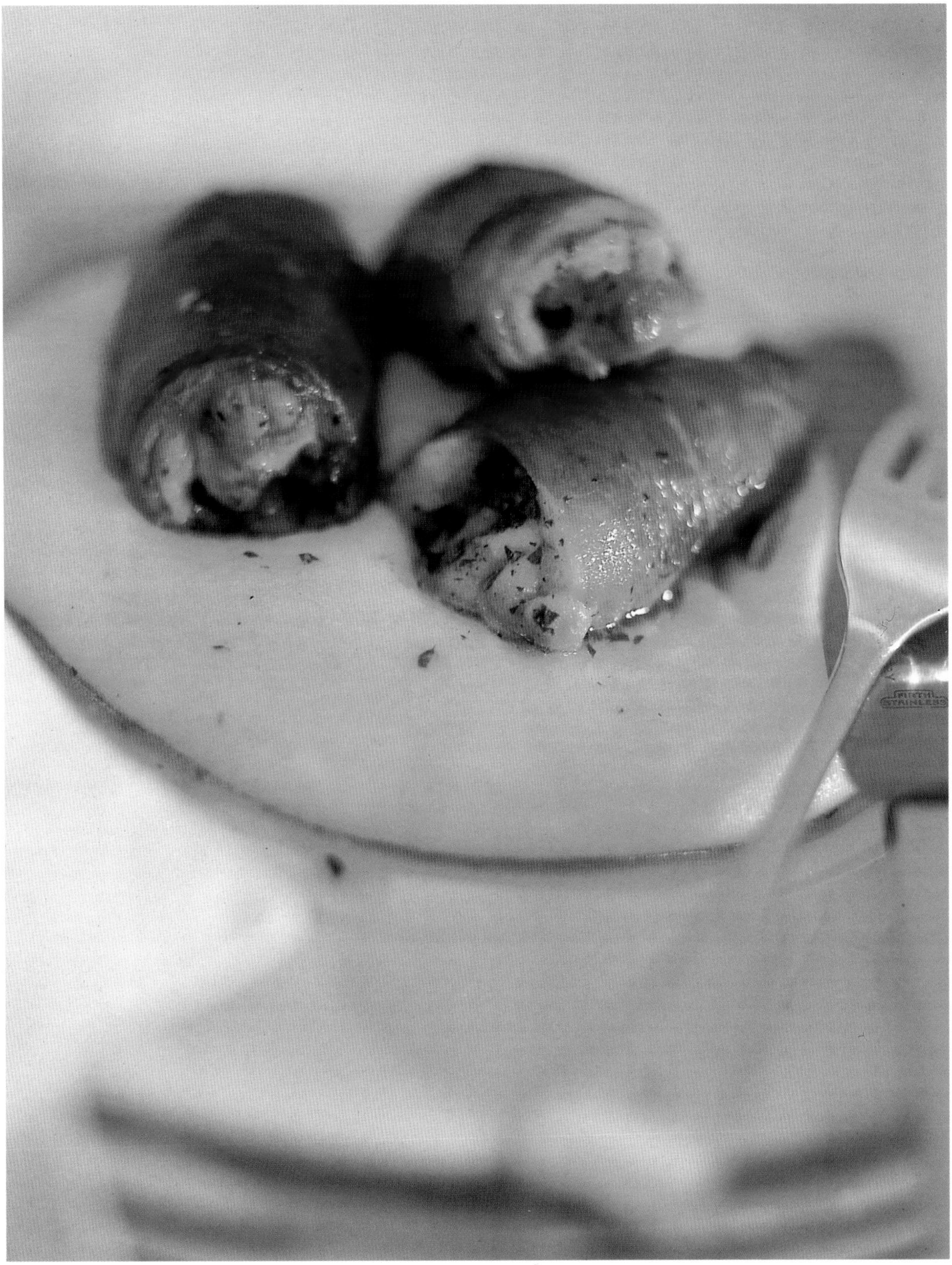

poached chicken with pancetta, sage and onion

Initial poaching of the chicken, followed by a brief roasting, delivers full-flavored, succulent meat with nicely crisped skin.

4 large chicken leg and thigh
   pieces
1 onion, quartered
1 large carrot, quartered
2 celery stalks, quartered
1 leek, quartered
6 parsley sprigs
2 bay leaves
¼ teaspoon peppercorns
12 thin slices pancetta
2 tablespoons olive oil

for the sage and onion sauce:
2 tablespoons butter
1 small onion, diced
2 tablespoons finely chopped
   fresh sage
1½ cups whole milk
6 thick slices white
   bread, crusts removed and
   made into bread crumbs
salt and pepper
1 tablespoon finely chopped
   parsley

serves 4

Cut the chicken into a large saucepan and pour over 3 quarts cold water. Bring to a boil and skim, then add the vegetables, parsley sprigs, bay leaves and peppercorns. Turn the heat down to a bare simmer and poach the chicken for 40 minutes. Turn off the heat and leave to cool in the liquid.

Preheat the broiler. Put the pancetta on a baking sheet and broil it until crisp. Remove and reserve.

Preheat the oven to 400°F. Remove the chicken from the stock and pat dry with paper towels.

Make the sage and onion sauce: melt the butter in a saucepan over low heat. Cook the onion gently until soft and translucent. Add the sage and stir in for a minute, then add the milk. Increase the heat to medium and bring to a boil. Turn the heat down to a simmer and stir in the bread crumbs. Cook for several minutes, season with salt and pepper and finish by stirring in the parsley.

Select a large ovenproof frying pan. Put it over high heat, add the olive oil and, when hot, lay the chicken in skin side down to color it for 1 to 2 minutes. Transfer to the oven for 5 minutes. The skin will finish browning while the meat heats through.

Put a large spoonful of the sauce on each of 4 warmed plates. Put the chicken on top of the sauce, skin side up, with the crisp pieces of pancetta on top.

slow-cooked chicken with coconut and whole spices

The chicken is cooked very slowly, allowing it to absorb all the flavors of the complex spice mix and the sweetness of the coconut milk. The jasmine rice makes a perfect accompaniment to the rich yet meltingly tender flesh and the spicy sauce.

4 chicken leg and thigh pieces, about 2¼ pounds total weight

2-inch piece fresh ginger, peeled and coarsely chopped

4 garlic cloves, coarsely chopped

2 red shallots, coarsely chopped

1¾ cup canned coconut milk (page 156)

2 teaspoons ground cumin

2 teaspoons ground coriander

¼ teaspoon ground turmeric

1 teaspoon salt

2 tablespoons sunflower oil

6 star anise

6 cardamom pods

6 dried red chilies

4 cloves

1 cinnamon stick

20 fresh curry leaves (or dried if fresh are unobtainable)

serves 4

Cut through the joint of the chicken legs to separate the drumsticks from the thighs and skin them.

Put the ginger, garlic and shallots into a blender or food processor with the coconut milk, cumin, coriander, turmeric and salt. Blitz to a fine liquid purée and reserve.

Put a heavy-based saucepan large enough to hold the chicken pieces in a single layer over medium heat and add the oil. When hot, add the star anise, cardamom pods, chilies, cloves, cinnamon and curry leaves. Fry, stirring, for 2 to 3 minutes, when they will have noticeably darkened.

Add one-third of the coconut milk mixture and allow to come to a boil, then add the chicken and turn to coat. As the liquid bubbles around the chicken, it will change in appearance and start to look oily. Continue to cook for 5 minutes, then add the rest of the coconut milk mixture. As soon as it returns to a simmer, turn the heat down and leave to cook, uncovered, for 1 hour. Stir frequently or it will stick and burn. Indeed, after 50 minutes, stir at 1-minute intervals. By now the chicken will be golden brown and most of the coconut milk will have evaporated, leaving an oily residue.

Pour away any remaining oil, leaving only the chicken and spices. Increase the heat to high, add 3 to 4 tablespoons of water and shake and stir to deglaze the pan. Transfer the chicken and the deglazed sauce to a serving bowl and serve with steamed jasmine rice (page 154).

marinated ginger poussins

The poussins, or small chickens, are spatchcocked before being marinated for 24 hours in a mixture of ginger and lemon juice. They may be cooked under an overhead grill [broiler] or on the barbecue. Poultry shears, while not essential, make preparing the birds very easy.

4 poussins

for the marinade:

7.5-cm / 3-in piece of ginger, thinly sliced

juice of 4 lemons

2 tbsp sunflower oil

2 tbsp light Chinese soy sauce

1 tsp chilli flakes

salt and pepper

serves 4

Cut the backbones out of the birds. Open them out and cut out the rib bones. Turn them over and flatten them with a blow to the breast.

Prepare the marinade: put all the ingredients except the salt and pepper in a blender or food processor. Blitz to an even texture. Put the birds in 2 ziplock bags and divide the marinade between them. Shake to coat and refrigerate for 24 hours, turning from time to time. Remove at least an hour before you want to start cooking.

Preheat the grill [broiler] to medium-hot. Remove the birds from the marinade and wipe dry with kitchen paper. Pass the marinade through a sieve, pressing with the back of a spoon, and reserve for basting.

Season the birds generously with salt and pepper and start to grill, skin towards the heat. Turn after 5 minutes, giving the meat side 5 minutes. Then brush with the marinade and continue to cook, basting and turning, for a further 5 minutes — 15 minutes in all (though you may judge they need a few minutes more).

Serve immediately with steamed jasmine rice (page 154).

braised duck with porcini

Like most dried wild mushrooms, dried porcini — also called cèpes — deliver a flavor out of all proportion to their dried weight. We tend to associate whole duck with roasting but here, after a preliminary browning, the bird is slowly braised in the oven.

1 duck, about 5½ to 6½ pounds
salt and pepper
1 ounce dried porcini
1 large carrot, coarsely
  chopped
1 yellow onion, coarsely
  chopped
3 garlic cloves, coarsely
  chopped
½ leek, white part only,
  coarsely chopped
1 celery stalk, coarsely
  chopped
3 fresh thyme sprigs
4½ cups strongly flavored
  chicken stock (page 152)
2 tablespoons Madeira
creamy mashed potatoes
  (page 69) or soft polenta
  (page 154), to serve

serves 4

Preheat an oven to 350°F. Wipe the bird all over with paper towels, then season, rubbing in the salt and pepper. Put the porcini to soak in ½ cup cold water.

In a large ovenproof dutch oven over medium heat, brown the duck all over until golden. The bird will release enough fat so you don't need to add any oil. Remove and reserve the duck while you add the vegetables and herbs and cook for 2 minutes. Put the duck back on top of the vegetables and pour over the stock. Bring to a boil, turn down the heat and simmer.

Remove the mushrooms from their soaking liquid, rinse and reserve. Line a sieve with cheesecloth or a coffee filter and strain the soaking liquid through it into the dutch oven. Add the Madeira. Put on the lid and put into the oven to braise for 2 hours, basting the duck from time to time.

Remove from the oven, transfer the duck to a serving dish and leave to rest for 10 minutes. Strain the braising liquid into a small saucepan and skim off the fat. Bring to a boil, lower the heat and simmer while you carve the duck. Pour any juice from the serving dish into the sauce.

Remove the legs and cut through the joint to separate drumsticks and thighs. Carve the breasts in thin slices and arrange on 4 warmed plates. Add the mushrooms to the sauce for a minute to warm them through, then spoon over and round the duck. Serve with the potatoes or polenta.

shichimi-spiced duck and escarole salad with ginger vinaigrette

Shichimi is an intriguing Japanese spice mix that is also called "seven-spice seasoning." It is hot with red pepper flakes and typically includes roasted sesame seeds, sansho pepper, dried orange peel, hemp seeds and roasted poppy seeds. You can buy it in small jars or packets from Japanese food shops. Escarole is a curly-leafed, slightly bitter-tasting salad leaf.

1 large whole duck breast, split
1 tablespoon sunflower oil
2 teaspoons shichimi (see above)
salt
1 head escarole, leaves
   separated
pepper

for the ginger vinaigrette:
salt and pepper
1 tablespoon rice vinegar
2-inch piece fresh ginger, peeled
   and sliced
4 tablespoons sunflower oil

serves 4

Brush the duck breasts with oil, then rub the shichimi mix into both sides with ½ teaspoon of salt. Leave for 30 minutes at room temperature to absorb the flavors.

Over low heat in a nonstick pan, place the duck breasts skin side down and cook for 10 minutes without moving them. Turn and give them another 5 minutes. Turn again, raise the heat and crisp the skin for 2 to 3 minutes. Transfer to a cutting board, skin side up, and leave for 10 to 15 minutes.

Put the escarole leaves into a large bowl. In a separate small bowl, make the dressing: dissolve ½ teaspoon salt and ¼ teaspoon pepper in the vinegar. In a small food processor, blitz the ginger with the oil. Pass through a sieve into the bowl with the vinegar, working as much of the pulp through as you can with the back of a spoon. Whisk to amalgamate, pour over the escarole and toss to coat.

Turn the duck skin side down and carve into thick slices at an angle. Mound the leaves on 4 plates and arrange the sliced duck on top.

4

barbecues

barbecues

The charcoal grill is among the most ancient of heat sources and the most modern—primitive in one sense, sophisticated in another. The grill is elemental and its application pure, apparently simple yet demanding acquired skill if it is to be used to best effect. A grill cook's judgment can only be based on experience. Precisely how hot a fire should be for different foods is a matter of empirical knowledge, for there are no thermostats or calibrated dials to provide precision. Heat must be judged by a hand held a few inches over the coals, and a squeeze bottle of water is the only way to lower the temperature. Inevitably, cooking over an open fire will result in flare-ups as fat drips and catches. Consequently, without an element of luck, perfect results cannot be expected first time, and factors beyond your control come into play. A strong wind will cause coals to burn faster and hotter, while the ambient temperature also affects thermal performance. Rain may not be an issue in an Australian or Californian high summer, but barbecue enthusiasts in less predictable climates know the depression a rolling swell of clouds casts over the happiest cookout.

In Australia most charcoal grills are home-built affairs made from bricks and with a solid cast-iron grill plate. They are fueled with dried hardwood, which is lit and allowed to burn down to glowing, smokeless embers before the food is cooked. Although the following recipes have been tested on the classic and most basic type of charcoal grill, many people prefer the more controllable options of an enclosed "kettle" form of barbecue or the gas-heated type with its permanent lava coals. Covered barbecues also provide opportunities for slow smoke cooking, the favored barbecue technique of the American Southwest, and can be used as ovens to cook large pieces of meat and whole poultry. This is particularly popular in places like Perth at the height of summer, when the heat makes kitchens without air-conditioning uncomfortable places to cook. Covered barbecues are available with both solid plates and bar grills. Solid plate grills are ideal for cooking marinated meats and poultry like Japanese teppanyaki or teriyaki dishes.

In this book we are only concerned with the simple charcoal grill, the universal cooking method of Southeast Asia and, with the obvious exception of a permanent brick grill, readily transportable. Japanese hibachi grills, for example, are great for picnics and have the benefit of three grill-rack positions; while disposable barbecues, though small, work perfectly well for skewered meat, fish and shellfish.

There are a number of constructive suggestions before beginning. Always clean out the ashes and start with a clean grill, plate or rack. A wire brush is the best way to get rid of burnt-on particles. Never be cheap with the charcoal, because the quality does make a difference. Often inexpensive fuel burns neither as hot nor as long as more expensive charcoal, suggesting that value can only be judged by performance and not by the price. The best charcoal is very light, so do not assume that a heavier bag is better value. It is more likely to suggest the addition of fillers.

A good depth of cooked coals is needed to deliver both sufficient heat and an extended cooking time. There are no absolute rules, but if you start by making a double layer of coals that extends beyond the cooking area by 3 inches and then build them into a pile before lighting them, they will burn down and distribute the right amount of heat for the desired grill area after burning for about 30 to 45 minutes. It is impossible to be any more precise, because different qualities of charcoal burn at different rates and achieve a different radiant efficiency. When ready, during daylight the charcoal will be gray with a powdery appearance, while at night it will give off a red glow.

The grill rack should be positioned 5 to 6 inches above the charcoal. After 30 or more minutes, extend a hand, palm downward, about 3 inches above the grill rack. If you have to snatch it away at once, it is almost certainly too hot for doing anything but searing meat or fish steaks to be

cooked tataki-style — that is, with a cooked exterior but raw in the middle. The skin of chicken exposed to this kind of temperature will burn to a bitter black long before the insides are done. If you can leave your hand above the heat for about 4 to 5 seconds, then you have achieved the temperature described in the recipes as medium-hot.

The charcoal grill, for so long identified with meat, is now as likely to be used to cook fish, a job for which it is ideally suited. This is not to say this is invariably easy, particularly when grilling whole fish. If they weigh more than 1½ pounds, it is easy to overcook the outer flesh before the flesh around the bones is done. The oiliness of the fish also makes a difference, with snapper, bass and mullet, therefore, more sensitive in this respect than salmon or mackerel. Small fish like sardines (page 90), which need the briefest exposure to the grill, are ideal candidates, as are shrimp. When cooking larger whole fish, a useful aid is a metal fish basket that allows you to turn the fish and remove it from the grill without damaging it. A similar basket for vegetables is also a good investment. Such baskets do need to be cleaned thoroughly between uses and oiled inside each time to prevent sticking, but if properly cared for they will have a long and useful life. Another way of cooking whole fish on the grill is in foil parcels (page 85), while putting a metal container like an upended roasting pan over the grill makes it possible to cook oysters, clams and mussels (page 89).

porgy with fennel and lemon

A foolproof technique for cooking whole fish on a barbecue is to contain them in a foil parcel. Aromatic fennel, garlic and lemon infuse the fish with flavor during cooking, while the foil reduces the fierceness of the grill's direct heat. An important part of the flavoring comes from the feathery tops of the fennel bulb, sometimes sold separately as a herb. Ask the fishmonger to scale, gut and clean the porgy for you.

Preheat the barbecue to medium-hot (pages 81–2). Cut off the feathery tops from the fennel and reserve. Cut the bulb into slices as thinly as you can manage.

Tear off a rectangle of foil large enough to wrap around one of the fish so that no juices escape during cooking. Brush with 1 teaspoon of the oil and season with salt and pepper. Place 2 slices of lemon in the center, then a quarter of the fennel slices and a quarter of the feathery fennel top and finally a quarter of the garlic. Season these aromatics with more salt and pepper, then place the fish on top. Season the fish and then sprinkle over a similar layer of the aromatics. Top with 1 teaspoon of oil and season again. Fold up the foil, bringing the edges to the middle then wrap over, crimping to seal. Prepare the second fish in the same way.

Place both packages on the barbecue and cook for 9 minutes, turn and give them a further 9 minutes. Transfer to a large oval plate, cut the parcels open down the center with a pair of scissors and pull the foil apart to present the whole fish. Finish by drizzling some oil on top.

1 small fennel bulb, with its
  feathery top
2 porgies, each about 12 ounces
4 teaspoons extra-virgin olive oil,
  plus extra for drizzling
salt and pepper
1 lemon, cut into 8 slices
1 garlic clove, sliced
  paper-thin

serves 4

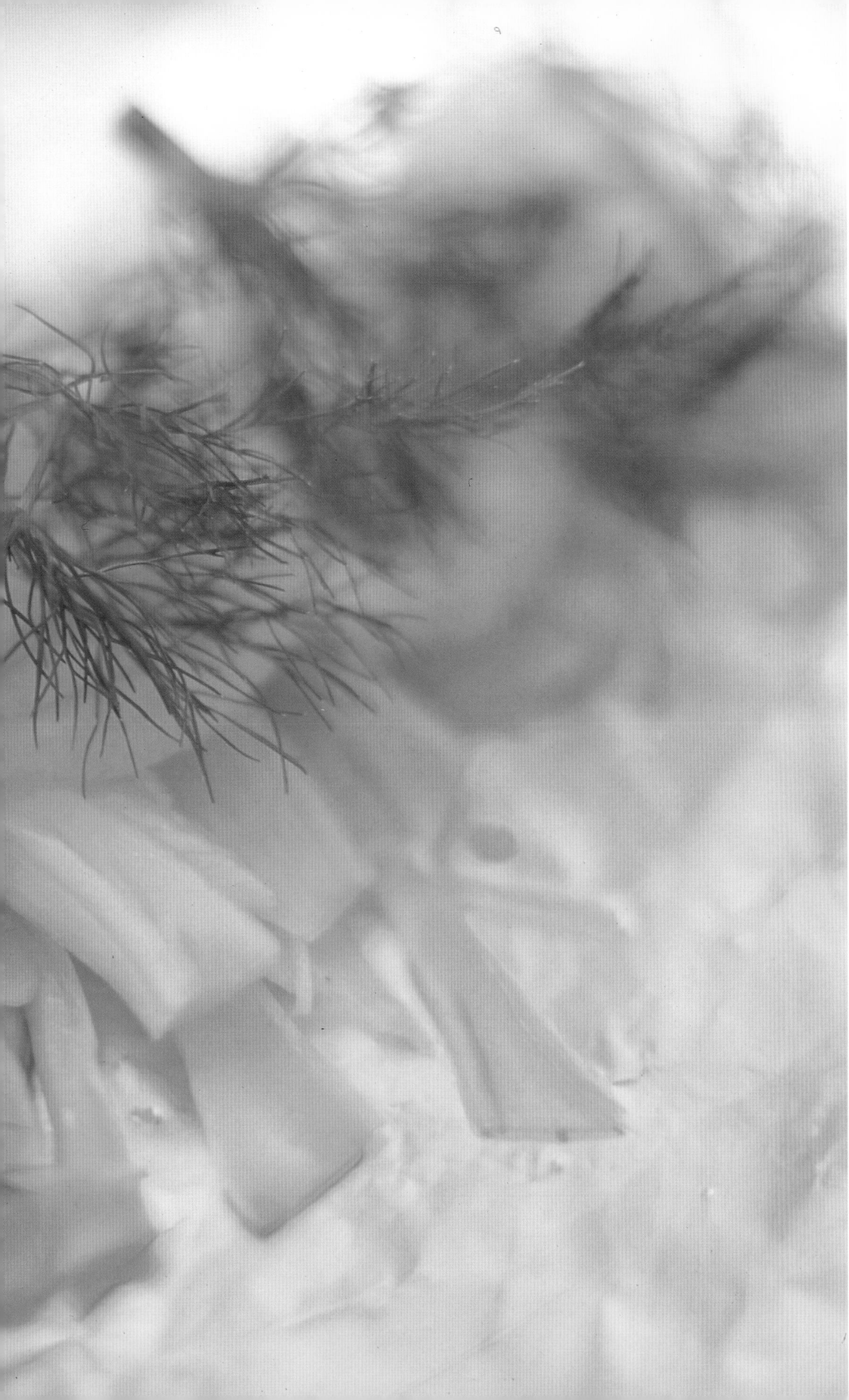

grilled swordfish with stewed red peppers and olives

Swordfish and tuna steaks are ideal for the barbecue or stove-top ridged grill pan. They involve a minimum of preparation time and are very easy to cook. All this dish needs to go with it for a perfect summer lunch is an arugula salad and a well chilled, crisp dry white wine.

4 swordfish steaks, each about
  6 ounces
1 tablespoon olive oil
salt and pepper
extra-virgin olive oil, to dress

*for the stewed red peppers
  and olives:*
2 red bell peppers
5 tablespoons olive oil
3 shallots, sliced
1 garlic clove, finely chopped
10 ounces ripe tomatoes, peeled,
  seeded and quartered
⅔ cup homemade tomato sauce
  (page 154) or canned thin
  tomato purée
salt and pepper
½ cup black olives, pitted

serves 4

First prepare the red peppers: preheat an oven to 475°F. Put the whole peppers in a roasting pan and drizzle a little olive oil over the top. Roast for 30 minutes, turning twice. Remove and leave to cool. When cool enough to handle, peel and seed, then cut into wide strips.

Put a saucepan over medium heat and add the remaining olive oil, shallots and garlic. Cook them slowly for 2 to 3 minutes, taking care not to allow them to color. Add the peppers, tomato quarters and tomato sauce or passata. Stir, turn down the heat and simmer gently for 30 minutes. Season with salt and pepper and remove from the heat to cool.

Preheat a ridged grill pan. Brush the fish steaks with the olive oil and season generously with salt and pepper. Lay them on the grill and cook for 4 minutes on each side. Transfer to a warmed plate and allow to rest for 2 minutes.

Reheat the peppers and stir in the olives. Place a large spoonful of the stewed peppers on 4 warmed large plates, followed by the swordfish steaks. Drizzle with a little extra-virgin olive oil and serve at once.

barbecued mussels with sweet chili vinegar

This technique for cooking mussels on the barbecue can be used with any shellfish. While 4¼ pounds sounds like quite a lot of mussels for 4 people, it usually only produces between 4 to 6 ounces of shelled meat, depending on the size of the mussels.

4¼ pounds mussels

for the sweet chili vinegar:
½ cup distilled white vinegar
7 tablespoons superfine sugar
2½ tablespoons lime juice
2 tablespoons fish sauce
**I small red chili, thinly
  sliced**
**I small green chili, thinly
  sliced**
2 shallots
**2-inches piece of cucumber, finely
  diced**
I tablespoon fresh cilantro leaves

serves 4

First make the dipping sauce: bring the vinegar and sugar to a boil in a pan, stir and remove from the heat. Leave until cool, then add the lime juice and fish sauce, the chilies, shallots and cucumber. Stir in the cilantro, transfer to a serving bowl and reserve.

Preheat the barbecue to medium-hot (pages 81–2). Put the mussels on the barbecue, cover with an upturned pan (or the lid if you have a kettle-type grill) and cook until they all open up. The mussels should cook in about 5 to 6 minutes. Depending on the size of your grill, you may need to do them in two batches.

Serve the mussels with the sweet chili vinegar as a dipping sauce.

salt-crusted barbecued sardines

The freshest fish needs only the simplest treatment to show it at its best. The barbecue is the perfect way to cook tiny sardines, which have enough natural oil to survive the rigors of a brief exposure to fairly fierce heat without drying. In Portugal this salt-crust treatment is common all along the coast and the fish are cooked ungutted, emerging plump and succulent with the salt and smoke taste from the barbecue perfectly balancing the richness of the just-cooked flesh.

You can grill slightly larger, gutted sardines this way but, if you do, experiment with one fish to judge the grilling time before cooking the rest. Cut it open after cooking for 2 minutes on each side to see if it is cooked down to the bone. If not, allow 3 minutes on each side when you do the rest.

24 ungutted small sardines,
  each about 1 ounce
coarse sea salt or kosher salt
olive oil
2 lemons, to serve

serves 4

Preheat the barbecue to medium-hot (pages 81–2). Rinse the sardines carefully under cold running water and lay to dry on paper towels. Crush the salt lightly (you don't want to powder it, just to eliminate the larger crystals). Sprinkle the salt liberally over the fish, turning to coat both sides.

Just before cooking, dip some paper towels in a little oil and wipe the barbecue rack with this to prevent sticking. Lay the fish on one at a time, working as quickly as you can, and give them 2 minutes before turning for a further 2 minutes on the other side (they don't need basting).

Remove the cooked sardines with a spatula, and arrange them 6 to a plate, with half a lemon on each plate. They need no further embellishment, just a glass of good white wine such as a crisp dry Muscadet or perhaps a Gewürztraminer Riesling to drink with them.

beef kofte with herbed bread

Kofte are Middle Eastern in origin: ground, highly spiced and seasoned meat pounded almost to a purée, formed into sausage shapes around wooden skewers and grilled. A labor-intensive process when using the traditional pestle and mortar, the food processor makes it easy and very quick. The *kofte* can be cooked on the barbecue or on a flat griddle over a gas flame. You can also shape the mixture into meatballs or make them into hamburgers and, if preferred, they can be made with lean ground lamb. Harissa, hot North African chili sauce, can be bought in small cans from most good food stores. Serve these *kofte* with warm dry-fried flat breads and *cacik*, a salad of cucumber, mint and yogurt.

1¾ pounds lean ground beef or
  ground lamb fillet
2 teaspoons cumin seeds
1 teaspoon coriander seeds
1 teaspoon red pepper flakes
½ teaspoon black peppercorns
½ teaspoon fenugreek powder
salt
6 fresh mint leaves
1 tablespoon chopped fresh
  cilantro
6 fresh basil leaves
2 tablespoons chopped fresh
  flat-leaf parsley
1 tablespoon olive oil
grilled flat bread (page 123),
  to serve
harissa, to serve

for the cacik:
½ cucumber, cut into ½-inch dice
2 garlic cloves, finely
  chopped
6 fresh mint leaves,
  finely chopped
1 small bunch fresh chives,
  finely chopped
1¼ cups thick yogurt
salt and pepper

serves 4 (makes 8 kofte)

The day before, soak 8 wooden skewers in cold water. This decreases the likelihood of their burning on the grill. Well ahead on the day of cooking, make the flat bread dough.

While the bread dough is rising make the kofte: put the cumin and coriander seeds, red pepper flakes and peppercorns in a small dry frying pan and toast over low flame for 2 to 3 minutes, stirring. Grind to a powder in a spice grinder and mix with the fenugreek and ½ teaspoon of salt.

Put the beef in a processor with the herbs, spices and olive oil. Blitz to a purée, then divide into 8 equal amounts. Roll these into balls, then into ¾-inch thick sausages. Mound these around the skewers and reserve.

Make the cacik: mix all the ingredients and season with salt and pepper. Cook the flat breads as described on page 123 and wrap them in a cloth to keep warm as they are cooked.

Grill the kofte, turning frequently until well browned on the outside but still pink in the middle, about 7 to 8 minutes.

Put a flat bread on each plate and place the kofte across the middle. Put a mound of cacik on one side and offer the harissa in a small bowl for people to help themselves.

grilled fillet of beef with candied shallots

Fillet of beef is the ideal candidate for a brief grilling on a very hot barbecue. It is shown at its best by the simplest accompaniments — creamy mashed potatoes (page 69) and shallots candied in butter and red wine.

4 pieces of beef fillet, each
about 6 ounces
1 tablespoon olive oil
salt and pepper

for the candied shallots:
2 tablespoons butter, softened
8 ounces shallots,
peeled and left whole
2 tablespoons superfine sugar
¾ cup red wine

serves 4

Preheat the barbecue to maximum temperature (pages 81–2). While it is heating, remove the beef from the refrigerator.

Make the candied shallots: put a heavy-bottomed frying pan over medium-high heat. Melt the butter and, when it sizzles, add the shallots and fry until brown all over. Add the sugar and allow the shallots to caramelize in it for 1 to 2 minutes. Then add the wine, turn down the heat and cook gently for 12 to 15 minutes, until there is only about 2 teaspoons of liquid left in the pan. Turn off the heat, but leave in the pan.

Brush the fillet steaks with the oil and season generously with salt and pepper. Lay on the now very hot grill and cook for 3 to 4 minutes on each side for a medium pink finish. If your preference is towards well done, give them 5 to 6 minutes a side. When the steaks are done to your liking, transfer them to a warmed plate while you reheat the shallots.

Tilt the plate to add any juices that run from the steaks into the shallots, shaking the pan to coat them. Spoon the candied shallots over the meat before serving.

beef with charred onions

Properly aged beef, which has been hung for several weeks in cold storage, is increasingly difficult to find. This is partly because of a universal trend toward centralized butchering of carcasses, with only selected cuts going Cryo-packed to individual shops, and because the process inevitably makes the beef more expensive. The price goes up because the cold storage space must be paid for and the meat loses moisture during the ageing, so the price increases by weight. It is significant that the Australian Meat & Livestock Commission says that beef exported by sea to Europe arrives beautifully aged as whole carcasses, being more tender and flavorsome after six weeks than when sold more immediately on the domestic market.

Note the instruction to season the beef heavily. You always do this when cooking on a barbecue or ridged grill pan because so much of it comes off. If you cannot get hold of any fresh horseradish, use commercially produced horseradish cream.

1 aged top round of
  beef, 2¼ pounds
about 5 tablespoons olive oil
salt and pepper
creamed horseradish or
  Dijon mustard, to serve

for the charred onions:
3 tablespoons olive oil
8 golf-ball–sized yellow
  onions, halved
1 garlic clove, chopped
¼ cup chopped fresh thyme

serves 4

Preheat the barbecue to medium-hot (pages 81–2) and the oven to 475°F.

Put a baking sheet over high heat and add 4 tablespoons of the olive oil. When hot, add the onions, cut surface down. Sear to color, season with salt and pepper and add the garlic and thyme. Turn after 4 to 5 minutes and cook the rounded side for the same time. Transfer to the oven to finish cooking for 40 minutes.

Twenty minutes before the onions are going to be done, brush the beef with a little olive oil and season heavily with salt and pepper. Put on the grill and cook for 5 minutes, then turn and give the other side 5 minutes. Turn twice more, giving a total of 20 minutes' cooking time to deliver a medium-rare finish. If you prefer it well done, give it another 5 minutes on each side. Transfer to a serving plate or carving board, cover with foil and leave to rest for about 10 minutes in a warm place.

Carve the rump into ½-inch slices and divide among 4 warmed plates. Pour over any meat juices and serve with the charred onions and creamed horseradish or Dijon mustard.

grilled veal chops with sage and roasted garlic

Deep-fried sage leaves make an interesting taste and textural counterpoint to the veal and roast garlic. Half a head of garlic per person sounds a lot but, after roasting, the garlic emerges sweet and surprisingly gentle.

2 small garlic cloves, plus 2 heads
  new season's garlic
5 tablespoons olive oil
1 tablespoon chopped fresh sage
  leaves, plus 1 cup sage leaves
salt and pepper
4 veal chops, each
  about 8 ounces
1 teaspoon paprika
1 cup sunflower oil
⅔ cup reduced chicken stock
  (page 152)

serves 4

Several hours ahead, put the veal to marinate: smash the 2 small extra garlic cloves and put them in a shallow dish with half the olive oil, the 1 tablespoon chopped sage, salt and pepper. Turn the chops in this and marinate at room temperature for several hours.

Preheat the barbecue and preheat the oven to 425°F.

Cut the heads of garlic in 2, slicing them laterally through the middle. Put these garlic circles cut side up in a roasting dish. Drizzle with some of the remaining olive oil, dust with paprika and season with salt. Bake for 30 to 40 minutes, basting once or twice as they cook. Remove and leave to cool.

Pour the sunflower oil into a deep-fryer and preheat to 375°F or heat the sunflower oil in a wok. Fry the whole sage leaves until crisp, then drain on paper towels.

Wipe most of the marinade from the veal chops and season both sides heavily with salt and pepper. Put them on the grill for 5 minutes, turn and cook the other side for a further 5 minutes. Remove and allow to rest on a warmed plate.

Bring the reduced stock to a boil in a small saucepan and add in any juices that have come from the chops.

Serve the chops on warm plates, spooning the stock mixture around them. Put a round of garlic on each plate and drizzle over the remaining olive oil; put a few sage leaves on top of each chop. Serve with a salad of mixed leaves, a combination that suggests a light Pinot might be a nice thing to drink with it.

barbecued lamb loin with roasted pumpkin and parsley

The lamb and roast pumpkin take about the same time to cook, so start to barbecue the lamb as soon as you have put the pumpkin in the oven. The only change to this recipe is that you peel the pumpkin. Ask your butcher to trim as much fat as possible from the lamb.

2 lamb loins, each
   about 14 ounces
1½ tablespoons olive oil
salt and pepper

for the roast pumpkin:
1 piece of pumpkin, 2¼ pounds,
   peeled and cut into
   1½-inch chunks
5 tablespoons olive oil
2 tablespoons butter, softened
2 tablespoons coarsely chopped
   fresh flat-leaf parsley
salt and pepper

serves 4

Preheat the barbecue to medium-hot (pages 81–2) and the oven to 475°F.

Cook the pumpkin: put the oil in a roasting pan over medium heat and, when shimmering hot, add the pumpkin chunks and season generously with salt and pepper. Turn the pumpkin pieces and, only as they start to color, put the pan in the oven and roast for 30 to 35 minutes, turning from time to time to ensure a uniform crisp brown surface.

As soon as the pumpkin goes into the oven, brush the lamb loins with olive oil and season well with salt and pepper. Put them on the grill and cook for 5 minutes. Turn and give the other side 5 minutes also. Turn again twice, to give a total of 10 minutes each side for a medium-rare, pink result. If you prefer it well done, grill for 5 minutes more on both sides, a total cooking time of 30 minutes. Remove and allow to rest for 5 minutes before carving, to allow the juices to move back to the center and give a much more tender result.

Remove the now caramelized pumpkin from the oven and crush the pieces gently together with a fork, adding the butter and parsley as you do so. Don't mash the pumpkin to a paste — it should still have discernible pieces. Taste and season with salt and pepper as liked.

Put a generous kitchen spoonful of the pumpkin on each of 4 warmed plates. Carve each loin into 8 thick slices, place 4 on top of each portion of pumpkin and serve at once.

barbecued spiced lamb with a red onion, tomato and lime salad

The use of yogurt as a tenderizing marinade is common throughout the Middle East and the Indian sub-continent. The spicing is quite subtle and therefore most appropriate for delicate spring lamb.

1 piece boned leg of lamb,
  about 2¼ pounds
juice of 1 lime
2 garlic cloves
heaping ¾ cup plain yogurt
½ teaspoon ground coriander
½ teaspoon ground cumin
½ teaspoon cayenne pepper
  or other ground chili
¼ teaspoon ground ginger
¼ teaspoon garam masala
salt

*for the red onion, tomato and
  lime salad:*
4 small red onions or 2 large
  red onions, thinly sliced
4 ripe plum (Roma) tomatoes,
  peeled and thinly sliced
3½ ounces fresh cilantro leaves,
  about 3½ cups, chopped
juice of 1 lime
½ teaspoon superfine sugar
pepper

serves 6

The day before: rub the lamb all over with salt and lime juice and leave for 2 to 3 hours at room temperature. In a bowl large enough to put the lamb, mix the yogurt with the spices. Peel and bruise the garlic with the flat of a knife thumped with the heel of your hand. Massage this mixture into the lamb and leave to marinate overnight in the refrigerator.

When ready to cook: preheat the barbecue to very hot (pages 81–2).

Make the salad: put the onions in a large bowl and add the tomatoes together with the cilantro leaves, the lime juice and sugar. Toss and grind over plenty of pepper.

Wipe off most of the marinade from the lamb with paper towels (left on, it will burn and produce a bitter crust). Grill the lamb for 8 to 10 minutes on each side, which will give a nicely charred finish with a pink-to-rare center. Leave to rest for 10 minutes, before carving across at an angle into ½-inch thick slices.

Arrange the slices on 4 warmed plates and serve the salad separately.

barbecued lamb steak with black olive butter

Most butchers sell lamb steaks cut from the leg, but you could buy a whole leg if catering for a large number and save money by doing so.

8 fresh rosemary sprigs
5 tablespoons olive oil
3 tablespoons port
salt and pepper
4 lamb leg steaks,
   each about 9 ounces

for the black olive butter:
½ cup unsalted butter, softened
1 tablespoon chopped fresh
   flat-leaf parsley
½ small garlic clove, very finely
   chopped
heaping ½ cup black olives,
   pitted and coarsely chopped
salt and pepper

serves 4

Several hours ahead, make the black olive butter: cream the butter in a mixing bowl, adding the parsley, garlic and olives. Season with salt and pepper and beat in. Scrape out onto a 10-inch square of parchment paper and roll this up, crimping both ends. Chill.

Bruise the rosemary. Put it in a shallow dish with the oil, port, a little salt and plenty of coarsely ground pepper. Turn the steaks in this mixture and cover with plastic wrap. Leave to marinate for several hours at room temperature.

Preheat the barbecue to medium-hot (pages 81–2). Wipe most of the marinade from the lamb and lay the steaks on the grill rack. Give them 5 minutes on each side, then transfer to a plate and allow to rest for 5 minutes.

Preheat a broiler. Cut 4 thick slices off the butter and put on top of the steaks. Flash them briefly under the broiler, removing them as soon as the butter starts to melt.

Put on warmed plates and serve with boiled new potatoes tossed in extra-virgin olive oil and a little red wine vinegar.

grilled lamb and red pepper pan bagnat

The *pan bagnat* is a Niçoise concept in which a loaf is filled and then pressed so that the bread absorbs the juices of the filling before it is cut. Here the filling is a charcoal-grilled lamb fillet cooked pink and sliced thinly, mixed with slices of roasted red pepper and the thinnest rings of raw red onion.

2 lamb neck fillets,
  each about 1 pound
1 tablespoon sunflower oil
salt and pepper
1 round ciabatta made
  with 1 pound dough (page 122)
4 oven-roasted red bell peppers,
  peeled and cut into strips
  (page 88)
1 red onion, very thinly sliced
1 garlic clove, sliced
6 fresh mint leaves
2 tablespoons extra-virgin
  olive oil

serves 4

Preheat the grill to medium-hot (pages 81-2). Brush the lamb with the sunflower oil and season generously with salt and pepper. In a heavy pan over high heat, sear the meat to brown it all over. Transfer to the grill and continue cooking for 12 to 15 minutes, when the meat will be medium-rare. Remove and leave to cool completely before carving into the thinnest slices you can manage.

Cut the loaf laterally through the middle. Lay the lamb on the bottom half and cover with the pepper strips, then the onion rings and garlic slices. Add the torn mint leaves, grind over some pepper and drizzle on the olive oil. Replace the top half of the loaf, put a board on top and weight with a couple of heavy cans. Leave for an hour, then cut into 8 wedges to serve.

skewered lamb fillet with eggplant and yogurt relish

2 lamb neck fillets,
  each about 1 pound
grilled flat breads (page 123),
  to serve
1 lime, quartered, to
  serve

for the marinade:
1½ teaspoons coriander seeds
½ teaspoon cumin seeds
1 large yellow onion, diced

Lamb fillet, the core of lean flesh attached to the neck end of the ribs, is a perfect cut for grilling. The roughly cylindrical shape of the fillet makes it easy to butterfly into a rectangular-shaped piece of meat about 1 inch thick, which can then be sliced lengthwise into strips. These are marinated with ground coriander seeds and lime juice, then threaded on skewers and grilled. The best way to make the most of a relatively small amount of marinade is to put it in a lock-top bag.

Soak 12 wooden skewers in water overnight or for several hours. At least 4½ hours ahead, prepare the meat and marinade: trim off any excess fat from the lamb fillets. For best effect you want to start with

juice of 4 limes
5 tablespoons olive oil
salt and pepper

for the eggplant and yogurt relish:
1 teaspoon black mustard seeds
½ teaspoon ground allspice
½ teaspoon black peppercorns
4 tablespoons
  extra-virgin olive oil
3 garlic cloves, cut into paper-
  thin slices
1 pound eggplants
½ cup fresh flat-leaf
  parsley leaves
juice of 1 lemon
heaping ¾ cup thick yogurt
salt

serves 4

as neat and compact a cylinder of meat as possible, so if they taper to a point at one end, cut this off and use for stew. Slice the fillets lengthwise down the middle, cutting along an imaginary line at the thickest point almost all the way through. Open the fillets along this cut and flatten them to make 2 rough rectangles. Cut these lengthwise into 6 equal strips to run the length of the skewer, making 12 in all.

Prepare the marinade: toast the coriander and cumin seeds in a dry pan over low heat for 3 to 4 minutes, then grind to a powder. Put the diced onion in a food processor with the lime juice. Blitz to a mush. The idea is to get as much liquid from the onion as possible. Pour through a sieve, pressing with the back of a wooden spoon, into a lock-top bag or a shallow dish with the meat. Add the ground spices, olive oil and seasoning (if using a dish, cover it with plastic wrap) and leave to marinate in the refrigerator for 4 hours. Bring to room temperature before continuing.

When you are ready to cook, preheat the grill to medium-hot (see pages 81–2). Thread the meat on the skewers and sit these across the top of a bowl to allow excess marinade to drip off.

Make the relish: toast the mustard seeds, allspice and peppercorns in a dry pan over low heat. Grind and set aside. Put the olive oil in the same pan together with the garlic. Cook gently over the lowest heat for 5 minutes, stirring from time to time (it must not brown). Add the spice powder and cook for a further 1 to 2 minutes.

Grill the eggplants, using a wire basket if you have it. Otherwise, turn frequently with tongs until the outside is blackened and blistered and the interior starts to soften. Leave until cool enough to handle and then peel, taking care to scrape off and discard any burnt flesh. Put the flesh into a food processor with three-quarters of the parsley. Blitz to a purée then, with the machine running at full speed, add the garlic mixture in a thin stream, followed by the lemon juice. Transfer to a bowl and stir in the yogurt. Add salt to taste and scatter the remaining whole parsley leaves on top.

Grill the lamb for 6 to 8 minutes, turning frequently. Halfway through, brush with the marinade and season generously. The outside should be nicely browned, the meat around the skewer still pink. While the lamb is cooking, grill the flat breads. Serve 3 skewers on each plate, with a quarter of the remaining lime, offering the hot bread from a basket and letting people help themselves to the relish.

marinated grilled chicken with oregano and lemon

In this quintessential barbecue dish, the chicken takes on a depth of flavor from the marinade and is cooked quickly on the grill.

4 skinless, boneless chicken
  breast halves
2 small garlic cloves
½ cup olive oil
1 teaspoon fresh oregano leaves
½ teaspoon fresh thyme leaves
¼ teaspoon grated lemon zest
salt and pepper
extra-virgin olive oil,
 to dress
lemon wedges,
  to serve

serves 4

Several hours ahead: remove the small fillets from the breasts (and use for another dish). Put the breast halves one at a time inside a lock-top bag and, on a good solid surface, gently beat them out with a meat bat or other heavy wooden implement to a uniform thickness of about ½ inch. Transfer to a plate when done.

Pour the olive oil into a large shallow dish or tray. Bash the garlic with the flat of a knife and add it to the oil with the herbs, lemon zest and some salt and pepper. Mix together well and turn the breasts in the mixture to coat them. Cover with plastic wrap and leave to marinate at room temperature for about 2 to 3 hours.

Preheat the barbecue or a stove-top ridged grill pan. Wipe most of the marinade from the chicken breasts. Sear and cook the chicken breasts for 2 to 3 minutes, turn and give the other side the same length of time.

Serve on warmed plates, drizzle with a little extra-virgin olive oil and put a lemon wedge on each plate. Serve with a large bowl of arugula with creamy mustard seed dressing (page 112).

grilled quail with muscatels

The quail are spatchcocked, that is the backbone removed and the birds flattened, before being marinated in an aromatic and sweet mixture of muscat and juniper berries. This ideally prepares them for the grill, while perfuming the flesh with an intriguing flavor.

You may want to ask the butcher to spatchcock the quail for you, or enjoy doing it yourself.

8 quail
6 juniper berries
2 tablespoons olive oil
salt and pepper

for the muscatel sauce:
3 tablespoons muscatel wine
scant ½ cup muscatel raisins
generous ¾ cup chicken stock
  (page 152)
1 tablespoon butter, diced

serves 4

About 1½ hours ahead: split the quail open down either side of the backbone, discarding the backbones, and flatten the birds with the heel of your hand. Make a small incision at the bottom of the breasts and thread the legs through it. Brush both sides with olive oil. Crush the juniper berries with the back of a knife to release their aromatic oil. Place the birds in a shallow dish and season with the crushed berries, salt and pepper. Leave at room temperature for 1 hour.

Preheat the barbecue for 30 minutes or so, to medium-hot (pages 81–2).

Make the muscatel sauce: warm the wine in a saucepan. Add the raisins and leave to macerate for 30 minutes. Strain through a sieve into another pan, reserving the muscatels, and reduce by half over medium heat. Add the chicken stock and bring to a boil. Lower the heat and simmer gently.

Put the quail skin side down on the grill for 3 minutes, turn and give the other sides 3 minutes also. Transfer to a warm plate and allow to rest for 5 minutes.

Turn the heat up under the sauce. Whisk in the butter and add the muscatels. Put the quail on 4 warmed plates and spoon the sauce over and round them.

vegetables 5

lasagne with ricotta, spinach and pumpkin

Unlike the traditional lasagne, which is baked, this version combines just-cooked ingredients at the last minute for a fresher effect and is served as individual portions. This is one of the few occasions in this book when it is suggested you use a microwave oven as part of the final preparation. You will therefore need a large flat serving plate that is microwave-safe — or ovenproof if using an ordinary oven — and which can also go under the broiler.

1 recipe quantity caramelized
  roast pumpkin (page 112)
1 recipe quantity pasta dough
  (page 151)
5 tablespoons fruity olive oil
2 tablespoons butter
1 garlic clove, finely chopped
14 ounces spinach
7 ounces ricotta cheese
5 tablespoons pecorino
  cheese, grated
salt and pepper

serves 4 as a main course

Preheat the oven to 475°F and cook the roast pumpkin (see page 112).

Make the pasta dough, rolling it out on the thinnest possible setting. Cut it into sixteen 4-inch squares. Bring a large pan of salted water to a rapid boil. Cook the pasta in this, 4 sheets at a time, for 3-4 minutes each batch. Transfer the pasta to a large bowl of cold water as it is cooked. When all are done, drain and lay in a single layer on a large plate or tray. Brush each lightly with a little oil to prevent sticking.

When the cooked pumpkin is cool, lightly crush it with a fork, adding 2 tablespoons of the olive oil as you do so.

In a wok or large frying pan over a high heat, melt the butter. Add the garlic, stir and immediately add the spinach leaves to wilt, a handful at a time. Season and drain well in a colander. Transfer to a mixing bowl, add the ricotta and 1 tablespoon of the grated pecorino and mix together well.

Place 4 sheets of pasta slightly apart on a heatproof plate that will fit in the microwave and under the broiler (see above). Cover with a layer of pumpkin, top each with a second sheet of pasta and layer with the spinach-and-cheese mixture. Put on the third pasta layer followed by more pumpkin, then the last sheet of pasta. Sprinkle over a little pecorino.

Preheat the broiler to maximum. Microwave the lasagne at full power for 1½ to 2 minutes. Transfer it to under the broiler and cook until the top starts to color.

Transfer the lasagne to warmed plates with a spatula. Drizzle with a little extra-virgin olive oil, scatter over the remaining pecorino and grind over some coarse pepper before serving.

chard and bean stew with celery leaves

This is more of a meal than just simply a dish and is similar to the Italian *ribollita*, featuring the dark-leaved cavolo nero and borlotti beans. This version uses Swiss chard and is best made in a large quantity. Lots of celery leaves are stirred in just before serving.

1¼ cups dried flageolet or other
  small pale green or white
  beans, soaked overnight
2¼ pounds Swiss chard
about 5 tablespoons olive oil
1 head celery
1 pound onions, diced
8 ounces carrots, diced
3 garlic cloves, thinly sliced
1⅛ pounds canned chopped
  tomatoes
salt and pepper
½ slightly stale baguette,
  crusts removed
about 3 tablespoon extra-virgin
  olive oil, plus extra to serve
1 cup fresh flat-leaf parsley
  leaves, coarsely chopped, to
  garnish

serves 6 as a main course

First prepare the beans: drain and rinse them, then place them in a saucepan and cover with water. Bring to a boil, turn down the heat and simmer for 25 to 30 minutes. Remove from the heat, drain and reserve the liquid.

Discard any damaged outer leaves from the Swiss chard and cut out and discard the stalks, then chop the leaves coarsely. Remove the strings from any tough outer celery stalks and dice the stalks; reserve the leaves.

Put the 5 tablespoons olive oil in a large pan and cook the chard, celery stalks, onions, carrots and garlic over low heat, stirring from time to time, for 20 to 25 minutes. Do not allow to brown. Add the tomatoes with their juices and continue to cook for about 30 minutes. Add half the beans and enough of their cooking liquid to cover, season with salt and pepper and simmer for another 20 minutes.

In a food processor, blitz the remaining beans to a coarse purée and stir this into the soup. Add the bread, torn into bite-sized pieces, and enough boiling water to achieve a spoonable soup consistency. Add the extra-virgin olive oil a tablespoon at a time, stirring in and tasting between additions, adjusting the seasoning if needed. Stir in the chopped reserved celery leaves

Serve in large bowls, with the parsley scattered over. Offer more extra-virgin olive oil at the table.

steamed chinese broccoli with sesame and oyster sauce

Chinese broccoli is deep green, with a long, fleshy stem, a few leaves, and a small head of flowers. When buying it, look for glossy, fresh-looking leaves. Also make sure the flowers have not started to sprout. Avoid tired, limp, yellowing vegetables that some Asian markets will try to unload on the unwary. Ask when they are expecting new stock and buy that day.

The technique of placing a bamboo steamer in a wok is both energy-efficient and traditional. If you have a metal Western-style steamer it can be used in exactly the same way and the cooking time will be the same.

This recipe works just as well with bok choy or choy sum. However, the cooking time will be slightly shorter.

14 ounces Chinese broccoli
1 tablespoon Asian sesame oil
2 tablespoons oyster sauce

serves 4

Remove any blemished leaves from the broccoli and trim the rest to the same size, keeping the stems, leaves and flowers attached.

Put 1 inch of water in a wok and bring to a boil. Put the trimmed broccoli in a bamboo steamer, cover with its lid and position over the water. Turn down the heat slightly and steam for 5 to 6 minutes, when the thickest part of the stems will be just cooked but still slightly crisp.

Remove the steamer from the wok and transfer the broccoli to a large bowl. Add the sesame oil and toss to coat. Put on a warm serving plate, cover with the oyster sauce and serve at once.

baked celery root with cream and parmesan

1 head celery root,
  about 2 pounds
1 tablespoon olive oil
1 small garlic clove, finely
  chopped
1 cup heavy cream
3 tablespoons milk
salt and pepper
2 tablespoons grated
  Parmesan cheese

serves 4

Preheat an oven to 400°F. Select an ovenproof dish about 10 x 6 x 2 inches in size. Put in the oil and garlic and rub to coat the dish all over.

Put the cream and milk in a large bowl, season with ¼ teaspoon salt and ¼ teaspoon pepper and stir in 1 tablespoon of the cheese.

Peel the celery root as you would a turnip or a rutabaga and cut in half. With the flat surface downward, cut it into very thin slices. Put half of the slices into the cream mixture and turn to coat. Remove one at a time, allowing excess to drip off before arranging in the dish, overlapping like roof tiles and building successive layers. Repeat with the second half, then pour any remaining cream mixture over and scatter over the remaining cheese.

Put into the oven and bake for 1 hour, when the surface will have glazed to a golden color while the celery root will have cooked all the way through to a creamy, moist finish.

baby beets in parmesan sauce

Baby beets make a delicious hot vegetable and are served here in a Parmesan-flavored sauce, a combination that goes well with any roast meat and is particularly good with chicken. The beets are best bought in a bunch with their leaves on but, if buying from a supermarket, they will have been trimmed. You can use ready-cooked beets, which will almost certainly be larger and come ready-peeled. If so, cut these into quarters before mixing into the sauce.

1½ pound baby beets
4 shallots, diced
2 tablespoons butter
3 tablespoons all-purpose flour
2½ cups whole milk
1¼ cups chicken stock
  (page 152)
1 bay leaf

Put a large pan of lightly salted water to boil. Scrub the beets and trim off the root and most of the leaf stem if necessary. Cook them hard in the boiling water for 30 minutes. Refresh in cold water and peel while still warm. Put into a gratin dish.

While the beets are cooking, in a heavy-based saucepan sweat the diced shallots in the butter until soft, then stir in the flour and cook, stirring, for 2 minutes. Whisk in the milk and chicken stock, add the

¼ teaspoon ground nutmeg

I cup grated Parmigiano
  Reggiano cheese

I tablespoon fine diced
  bread crumbs

salt and pepper

serves 4

bay leaf and nutmeg, season lightly with salt and pepper and bring to a boil. Lower the heat to a bare simmer and cook for 25 minutes, stirring at regular intervals and paying particular attention to the edges, where the sauce tends to stick and burn.

Preheat a hot broiler. Stir most of the grated cheese into the sauce, reserving I tablespoon. Continue stirring until the cheese melts into the sauce, then pour over the beets.

Mix the remaining cheese and bread crumbs together and scatter over the top of the beets. Put briefly under the hot broiler until you have a gratin finish to the surface.

creamy baked eggplant with tomato and parsley

I eggplant, about I0 ounces, cut
  into ¼-inch-thick slices

2 teaspoons olive oil, plus more
  for brushing

½ small yellow onion,
  finely chopped

½ garlic clove, finely chopped

I teaspoon lemon juice

I¼ cups heavy cream

salt and pepper

3 tablespoons tomato vinaigrette
  (page 153)

2 tablespoons chopped fresh
  flat-leaf parsley

serves 4

Arrange the eggplant slices on a baking sheet, sprinkle with salt and leave for 20 minutes, which will cause drops of water to form as moisture is drawn from the flesh. Brush off all the salt and dry the slices with paper towels.

Preheat an oven to 350°F.

Put the oil in a small saucepan over a medium heat and, when hot, add the onion and garlic. Sweat for 2 minutes, stirring. Add the lemon juice, followed by the cream and bring to a boil. Lower the heat and simmer for 2 minutes. Season with salt and pepper and remove from the heat.

Put a ridged grill pan over high heat. When hot, brush the eggplant slices on both sides with the smallest amount of oil and grill for about I minute each side. Transfer to a tray.

Pour a little of the sauce onto a shallow, ovenproof serving dish and spread it around with a large spoon. Lay the eggplant slices on top, not overlapping. With a teaspoon, spread a little of the vinaigrette on top of the eggplant slices, then pour the remaining sauce around the slices. Mill over plenty of pepper and bake for 10 minutes.

Remove from the oven, scatter over the parsley and serve immediately.

caramelized roast pumpkin

Roast pumpkin is a standard vegetable accompaniment to the Australian Sunday roast meat.

1 piece pumpkin, 2¼ pounds
5 tablespoons olive oil
salt and pepper

serves 4

Preheat an oven to 475°F. Leave the skin on the pumpkin, remove and discard the seeds and cut the flesh into 1½-inch chunks.

Put the oil in a roasting pan placed over medium heat and, when shimmering hot, add the pumpkin chunks and season generously with salt and pepper. Turn the pumpkin an , only as it starts to color, put the pan in the oven and roast for 30 to 35 minutes. Turn from time to time to ensure a uniform crisp, brown surface. Before removing from the oven, check it is properly cooked by inserting a fork into the largest piece. It should be crisp on the outside and meltingly soft but still coherent in the interior. Serve immediately.

arugula with creamy mustard seed dressing

The clean, peppery taste of arugula is best complemented by a forceful dressing. The amount of dressing given here is double the quantity you need. It keeps well in a jar in the refrigerator.

7 ounces arugula

for the creamy mustard seed
  dressing:
4 teaspoons Dijon mustard
¼ teaspoon yellow
  mustard seeds
1 egg
2 teaspoons cider vinegar
salt and pepper
½ cup peanut oil
1 tablespoon mayonnaise

serves 4

First make the dressing: in a bowl, whisk together the Dijon mustard, mustard seeds, egg, vinegar, ½ teaspoon of salt and ¼ teaspoon of pepper. Then slowly whisk in the oil, pouring in a thin stream until fully homogenized. Whisk in the mayonnaise and, finally, 4 teaspoons warm water, a teaspoon at a time. Taste and adjust the seasoning if needed.

Put the arugula leaves in a bowl and toss to coat in half the dressing. Transfer to a serving bowl, mounding the dressed leaves and finishing with a few turns of coarsely ground pepper.

fried tempeh with long beans and kecap manis

Tempeh, akin to tofu and also made from soy beans, is used extensively in the Asian kitchen. It is completely vegetarian, yet high in protein. You can buy it from Asian and health-food shops. Long beans, also known as snake beans and yard-beans, are long just as their name suggests — 12 to 16 inches — and look like an oversized green bean. They can be found in Asian markets in and around Chinatowns, but you could substitute green beans.

14 ounces tempeh
⅓ pound long beans
2 garlic cloves
2 small red shallots

Cut the tempeh into 1-inch cubes. Top and tail the beans and cut into 2-inch pieces. Cut the garlic and shallots into thin slivers and the onion into thin rings.

1 red onion

3 tablespoons sunflower oil

2 tablespoons kecap manis

2 tablespoons fish sauce

serves 4

Heat the oil in a wok over medium heat and, when hot, fry the tempeh for 30 seconds, turning to brown. Remove and transfer to a dish lined with paper towels to drain.

Pour off all but 1 tablespoon of the oil. When this is hot, fry the garlic and shallot gently for 2 minutes, taking care not to allow them to color. Add the beans and fry for 4 minutes, tossing and stirring from time to time to keep the beans turning as they cook.

Add the onion, stir in and cook for 1 minute. Return the tempeh to the wok and mix everything together well. Add the kecap manis and fish sauce, toss and transfer to a warmed bowl to serve.

spicy bulgur pilaf

Bulgur, sometimes spelled bulghur or burghul, can be eaten in its usual partly processed state in a salad (see Tabbouleh, page 32) or cooked, as in this pilaf, which can accompany either confit of duck or braised chicken equally well.

1⅓ cups bulgur

3 tablespoons sunflower oil

1 small yellow onion, finely
   chopped

1 garlic clove, finely
   chopped

1 red chili, seeded and
   finely diced

½ teaspoon salt

¼ teaspoon pepper

2 cups chicken stock (page 152)

1 tablespoon fresh flat-leaf
   parsley, chopped

1 tablespoon fresh thyme leaves

serves 4

Soak the bulgur in lots of cold water for 2 minutes, then drain through a sieve and reserve.

Select a saucepan with a tight-fitting lid and put it over medium heat. Film the base with the oil, add the onion, garlic and chili and cook for a minute, stirring with a wooden spoon. Add the bulgur and turn to coat for 2 minutes. Season with the salt and pepper and pour over the chicken stock. Bring to a boil, stir once more, turn down to the lowest heat and put on the lid. Simmer gently for 40 minutes.

Turn off the heat and leave with the lid on for 10 minutes, then stir in the herbs and serve.

jerusalem artichokes in olive oil with herbs and spices

This very Middle Eastern treatment delivers a delicious and unusual vegetable accompaniment to have with roast fish, on bruschetta or as an antipasto in its own right. Fennel can be braised in olive oil in the same way. Before serving, remove the artichokes from the refrigerator and allow them to come to room temperature.

1⅛ pounds Jerusalem artichokes
2 lemon zest strips, plus
   the juice of ½ lemon
3 garlic cloves
1 red chili
4 bay leaves
¼ teaspoon peppercorns
¼ teaspoon coriander seeds
5 sprigs each fresh
   oregano and thyme
1 teaspoon salt
3½ cups olive oil

serves 4

Peel the Jerusalem artichokes and put immediately into water acidulated with the lemon juice to prevent discoloration.

Drain and put them into a pan with all the other solid ingredients, then pour the olive oil over. Bring to a boil, immediately lower to a bare simmer and cook for 25 minutes. Test with a knife blade, which will slide in easily when done.

Leave to cool completely before packing into a jar, pouring over the aromatic cooking liquid and storing in the refrigerator. The preparation will develop in flavor after about a month or so.

baked pink fir apples with garlic, thyme and cream

Pink Fir Apples are lovely waxy potatoes characterized by an unusual, knobbly appearance, pink-blushed skin and distinctive flavor. Any similar new potato can be used here.

2¼ pounds Pink Fir Apple or
   other new potatoes
2 garlic cloves
1¼ cups heavy cream
2 teaspoons fresh thyme leaves

Preheat an oven to 350°F.

Wash, peel and dry the potatoes. Peel the garlic and bruise with the back of a knife. Put in a saucepan with the cream and thyme and bring slowly to a boil. Immediately remove from the heat and leave to cool and infuse.

salt and pepper

1 tablespoon grated
  Parmesan cheese

1 tablespoon chopped fresh
  flat-leaf parsley

serves 6

Cut the potatoes lengthwise into ¼-inch-thick slices and stir into the cream. Season with salt and pepper. Layer the slices carefully in a small 2-inch-deep baking dish, allowing excess cream to drip back into the pan. Repeat until you have used up all the slices. Pour over the remaining cream and scatter the Parmesan over the top.

Cover with foil and bake for 40 minutes. Remove the foil and turn the oven up to 425°F. Bake for a further 40 minutes, when the surface will be a rich golden brown. Remove from the oven, scatter over the parsley and serve at once.

fried potatoes with thyme, bay and lemon

The kind of potato you use here is vital to the quality of the finished dish. In Australia, Tassi Golds would be a good choice, a waxy variety with a bright, golden flesh and a lovely flavor. Yukon Gold or Yellow Finn would work well, too.

1¾ pounds waxy potatoes,
  scrubbed but unpeeled
  (see above)

½ cup olive oil

3 garlic cloves

6 fresh thyme sprigs

2 bay leaves

½ teaspoon grated lemon zest

salt and pepper

2 tablespoons butter,
  softened and diced

1 teaspoon chopped fresh flat-
  leaf parsley

serves 4 to 6

Put the potatoes in a pan and cover with salted water. Bring to a boil, turn down the heat and simmer for 15 minutes. Remove from the heat and leave to cool in the water before draining.

Pour the olive oil into a large flat-bottomed dish. Smash the garlic and add to the oil, followed by the thyme, bay leaves, lemon zest, 1 teaspoon of salt and ½ teaspoon of pepper. Cut the potatoes in half and lay them, cut side down, in the oil. Baste and leave to marinate at room temperature for 2 to 3 hours.

Heat a large, heavy-based frying pan over medium-high heat. You want the potatoes to fry in a single layer (use 2 pans if necessary). Remove the potatoes from the marinade and pour and scrape it into the pan. As it starts to sizzle, lay the potatoes in, cut side down. Fry gently for 5 to 6 minutes, allowing them to take a strong golden color, then turn them over and continue to cook for 2 to 3 minutes. Transfer to a warmed serving dish, cut side up.

Scatter over the butter, then pour over the contents of the pan. Sprinkle over the parsley and a little more salt before serving.

okra with red onions and sambal

Many people don't like okra — also called bindi (Indian) — because they have only eaten it after lengthy cooking as in, for example, a Louisiana gumbo, when it can sometimes go gelatinous and slimy. Indian and Southeast Asian treatments usually give a preliminary soaking in cold water, while only cutting the okra immediately before a relatively brief cooking delivers a beautifully crisp and fresh green vegetable.

8 ounces small okra
2 tablespoons sunflower oil
5 ounces red onions,
  thinly sliced
2 tablespoons Balinese chili
  sambal (page 48)
¼ teaspoon turmeric
½ teaspoon fish sauce
2 teaspoons kecap manis
  (page 156)

serves 4

Soak the okra in a bowl of cold water for 1 hour. This has the dual benefit of cleaning them and making them crisp when cooked. Drain in a colander and leave to dry for 5 minutes.

Put the oil in a wok over medium heat and, when hot, stir-fry the onion for 2 to 3 minutes, or until soft but not colored. Add the sambal and stir-fry for 30 seconds.

Top and tail the okra and add with the turmeric. Fry, tossing, for 3 to 4 minutes, adding the fish sauce and kecap manis toward the end of cooking. Serve at once.

cabbage and potatoes with pancetta

The way to keep green vegetables as brightly colored as possible is to put them into the pan as soon as the water achieves a rolling boil. Putting a lid on means the water will return to a boil more quickly. As soon as the water is boiling again, remove the lid. Check the greens from time to time, so you can remove them from the heat the instant they are done. The result will be a bright-green vegetable that tastes as good as it looks.

2¼ pounds young cabbage,
  cavolo nero or
  Savoy cabbage
2¼ pounds floury potatoes,
  peeled
8 ounces pancetta
  or bacon, in 1 piece
scant ¾ cup butter, softened
3 tablespoons whole milk
salt and pepper

serves 6-8

Separate the leaves from the cabbage, cut away the thick stalks and slice the greens finely. Select a large saucepan with a tight-fitting lid, fill with salted water and bring to a boil. At the same time in another pan, bring the potatoes to a boil in salted water and cook for 20 minutes.

As soon as the water for the greens reaches a rolling boil, add the shredded leaves and put the lid back on. Return to a boil and cook for 5 to 10 minutes, drain in a colander and allow them to dry off.

Preheat a broiler. Cut the pancetta or bacon into ¼-inch-thick slices and broil them, turning, until browned on both sides. Remove, reserving the fat that has rendered during cooking. When cool, chop the pancetta or bacon coarsely and reserve.

When the potatoes are cooked, drain and leave to dry off. Return to the pan and mash by hand, reducing to a coarse purée. Add the butter and greens, followed by the pancetta or bacon and beat together well. Still beating, slowly add the milk and season with salt and pepper.

Spoon the potato mixture into a warmed bowl. Quickly reheat the rendered fat and drizzle over the top. Serve at once.

6

breads & cookies

ciabatta

Most white bread benefits from the use of high-protein bread flour. Ciabatta, often thought to be beyond the reach of the private cook, is surprisingly easy to make if you break the rules and use dough that has been given a lengthy secondary rising time in the refrigerator. This recipe can be used immediately, without the chilled rising, to make a closer-textured bread, or rolled out thinly for pizzas.

1 envelope active dry yeast

1 teaspoon sea salt

½ teaspoon superfine sugar

1 tablespoon olive oil, plus more
   for brushing

6½ cups strong white wheat
   bread flour, plus more for
   dusting

makes 2 ciabatta loaves

Ideally the day before, put 2½ cups of hand-warm water in the bowl of a stand mixer with the yeast, salt, sugar and oil. Pour in the flour and, using the dough hook and starting at the lowest low speed, work for 8 to 10 minutes. If the dough is not holding and is still pulling apart in strands, add more water a tablespoon at a time until it does. Increase the mixer to full speed for 1 minute, when you will have an elastic dough that is resilient and springy. If the dough is too sticky, shake in a little more flour and work for 30 seconds to incorporate it. If too hard or not forming a coherent mass, add another tablespoon of water, switch on and work in until it does.

Turn the dough out on a well-floured surface, knock down and shape into a ball. Brush with a little oil and put in a lightly oiled bowl large enough to allow the dough to treble in size. Cover the top loosely with plastic wrap and leave to rise in a fairly cool and draft-free environment. If you leave dough to rise in a hot place it will do so in a spectacular and rapid way, but will produce a heavier loaf. Leave for at least 2 hours and up to 3, when the dough should have risen above the top of the bowl in a sticky and elastic mass.

Transfer the dough to a heavily floured surface, punch down and knead by hand for 2-3 minutes. It could now be baked as pizza but for ciabatta, divide in half. Put the large pieces in lock-top bags and refrigerate for 24 to 36 hours . Remove from the refrigerator an hour before you want to bake. This will produce a fine, crisp crust and a light interior.

Preheat an oven to 475°F. Take the dough out of the bags, dust with flour as they will be sticky and pull gently into ovals that fit into non-stick jelly-roll pans or heavy-duty baking sheets. Cover with clean cloths and leave to rise for 45 minutes.

Spray the oven with water, close the door and leave for 30 seconds to generate steam. Then put in the loaves and bake for 30 to 35 minutes, turning the temperature down to 425°F for the last 10 to 15

bread & cookies

grilled flat bread

1½ teaspoons active dry yeast
1 teaspoon sea salt
½ teaspoon superfine sugar
1½ teaspoons olive oil
3¼ cups bread flour, sifted
1 tablespoon chopped fresh
  cilantro
2 green onions, thinly sliced
oil for greasing

makes 4

Well ahead, put 1¼ cups hand-warm water, the yeast, salt, sugar and oil in the bowl of a stand mixer. Using the dough hook and starting at low speed, pour the sifted flour into the liquid and work for 8 to 10 minutes. Increase to full speed, add the chopped cilantro and green onions and work for another minute until elastic and a little sticky. If too resistant to the touch, turn on again and add 1 to 2 tablespoons of water and work for a minute to amalgamate.

Transfer to a floured surface, knead for a minute or two, form into a ball and put in a lightly oiled bowl large enough to allow it to more than double in bulk. Brush the top with oil and wrap the top of the bowl in plastic wrap. Leave to rise in a draft-free place for 2 hours. Do not put in a hot place, for example, next to the oven to force this process as the slower the rise, the lighter the bread.

Preheat a griddle or barbecue to medium-hot (see pages 81–2). If using a barbecue, put a heavy metal sheet on top of the grill. Punch down the risen, moist and sticky dough on a floured surface. Knead for a minute or two, then divide into 4 pieces and roll each into a 9-inch round.

Cook the rounds on the griddle or barbecue, pushing them down with a spatula to encourage the air in them to balloon the bread in the middle and give a lighter finish. Cook for about 2 minutes, until the bottom is speckled brown. Flip them over and give the other side 2 minutes. If necessary, wrap in a cloth to keep them warm before serving.

pistachio and herb bread

If you are fortunate enough to have a local baker who produces good baguettes, this is a quick and easy way of making a delicious snack to have with drinks.

1 baguette
scant ¾ cup unsalted butter,
  softened
2 tablespoons chopped
  fresh basil
1 tablespoon chopped
  fresh flat-leaf parsley
½ teaspoon chopped fresh thyme
1 garlic clove, finely chopped
scant ½ cup unsalted
  pistachio nuts
1 egg yolk
salt and pepper

serves 4 to 6

Preheat a broiler. In a mixing bowl, cream the softened butter with a wooden spoon for 2 minutes. Beat in the basil, parsley, thyme and garlic.

In a food processor, blitz the pistachios to a coarse crumb, then mix evenly into the butter. Add a few turns of black pepper and beat in the egg yolk.

Cut the baguette at an angle into long slices about 1 inch thick. Spread these generously with the butter and put under the grill until cooked and colored.

The pistachio and herb butter will keep for a week to 10 days in the refrigerator, but no longer as it goes moldy. It may also be frozen.

banana bread

One of the problems bananas share with tomatoes, avocados and many other fruits is that even when picked they continue to ripen, and markets always sell them still unripe when the skins are pale yellow tinged with green and the flesh inside hard and tasteless. Only when the bananas start to fleck with brown will they be sweet, soft and ready to eat. At this point they do not last for long and move rapidly to a blackened over-ripeness. It is just before this point that bananas are perfect for making bread.

½ cup unsalted butter
⅔ cup raw sugar
  such as demerara
1 egg
2 or 3 very ripe bananas (about
  1 cup mashed)

Preheat an oven to 350°F.

Cream the butter and sugar, then beat in the egg. Mash the bananas and mix with the sour cream, then beat this into the creamed sugar and butter. Sift the flour into the mixture and add a pinch of salt, stirring and folding in gently. Spoon into a nonstick 2-pound loaf pan

⅔ cup sour cream
1⅔ cups self-rising flour
pinch of salt

makes one 2-pound loaf

(9 by 5 inches), cover with foil and bake for 1 hour. Remove the foil to allow the top to color and return to the oven.

After a further 20 minutes, check the loaf by inserting a skewer into the middle. When it comes out warm and clean, the banana bread is done. Leave for 10 minutes before turning out onto a wire rack to finish cooling.

fruit-and-nut loaf

This tasty bread makes a rich and sweet counterpoint to soft ripe Brie, Camembert, Taleggio and other creamy soft cheeses. It is also very good simply spread with butter.

vegetable oil or butter for
  greasing
⅔ cup unprocessed bran
1 cup whole milk
scant 1¼ cups self-rising flour
¼ teaspoon salt
½ cup dried currants
½ cup golden raisins
⅔ cup walnuts, broken into
  pieces
½ cup golden syrup

makes one 900-g / 2-pound loaf

Preheat an oven to 350°F. Line a 2-pound loaf pan (9 by 5 inches) with parchment paper and grease lightly with vegetable oil or butter.

In a large mixing bowl, soak the bran in the milk for 5 minutes. Sieve in the flour and salt and mix in thoroughly. Then add the fruit, walnuts and golden syrup. Mix together to amalgamate uniformly.

Pour this very moist mixture into the prepared pan and bake in the center of the oven for 1¼ hours.

Allow to cool on a wire rack, then turn out of the pan. Wrap in parchment paper and keep in an airtight container if not eating at once. Cut into slices about ¼ inch thick to serve.

coffee in a café society

Australia has taken to coffee with a vengeance, and its cities would seem to have more cafés than pubs these days. Of course, they don't serve any old coffee but the finest espresso and the very contemporary manifestations: cappuccino, caffè ristretto, caffè lungo, doppio espresso, caffè macchiato, caffè latte, latte macchiato and caffè mocha, all based on espresso coffee and, as is proper with a coffee-making system which originated in Italy, described in Italian. Everything depends on the quality and blend of Arabica and Robusta beans that produce the perfect balance of bitter, acid and sweet elements in the cup, the extraordinary aroma, the complex flavor and the hazel-colored *crema* on the surface that always tops a perfect espresso.

The espresso machine first became popular in Europe in the second decade of this century, *espresso* meaning "on the spur of the moment" to identify the immediate nature of the product. The principle of the system — which forces water at 195°F under pressure through individual portions of finely ground coffee for between 20 and 30 seconds — remains unchanged. The ease of use and efficiency of the mechanism have gotten better, but we would recognize Bezzeria's first commercially produced machine of 1901 as the precursor of the Gaggia, with its distinctive pump handles, which completely revolutionized coffee drinking when introduced in 1945 and was to be found in coffee bars the world over in the fifties. Today we can buy small espresso machines for domestic use. When these were first introduced, lack of pressure in the *vapore*, the wand that steam-whips milk to produce the distinctive frothy and creamy top of a cappuccino, meant poor results.

There are a number of things to take into consideration to get the best results when steam-whipping milk. As a general rule, the lower the fat, the greater the froth; but with technical improvements in frothing attachments, this is no longer as significant as it used to be. Milk froths best in a metal pitcher and in one that is wider at the base than at the top. The temperature does matter and you should always start with cold milk from the refrigerator. As you apply the steam, the hotter the milk gets the less it froths. For this reason Italians have always drunk cappuccino warm rather than hot and, incidentally, never after 11 a.m. This rule does not of course apply outside of Italy, where milky coffee is now popular even after dinner.

espresso and variations on the theme A classic espresso is made with ¼ ounce of finely ground coffee and 3 tablespoons water. It is served in a demitasse, a heavy cup that holds 4 tablespoons and should be warmed before use. Cafés usually stack cups on top of the espresso machine to warm them, but the easiest thing to do at home is to rinse them with boiling water. The *crema* you achieve will be an indicator of how well balanced the roast is and whether the grinder setting is correct.

* A cappuccino is properly made with caffè ristretto, that is a very strong espresso made with 2 tablespoons of water and ½ cup of frothed milk. It is served in a standard-sized coffee cup. The froth should stand proud of the rim and have a white center surrounded by a discernible ring of *crema*.

* Caffè macchiato is an espresso with a spoonful of milk froth on the top.

* A doppio espresso is simply a double helping of espresso in a larger cup.

* Caffè lungo is a diluted espresso made with twice the amount of water.

* In Italy, caffè latte is made from an espresso and only slightly frothed milk. The two are combined in a large cup or glass by being poured into it at the same time. This is drunk exclusively at breakfast.

* In Australia and the US, caffè latte is made with more milk than in Italy — as much as 350 ml / 12 fl oz [1½ cups] — and is invariably served in a glass. The Italian description for this is latte macchiato, which means 'stained milk'.

preserved sugared figs

The sugar sounds excessive, but the technique is the classic French way of candying fruit and the figs should be barely ripe. Ideally you should candy fruit in the summer, when they can be dried in the sun, but they will finish perfectly well in a warm kitchen. The breeze from a fan helps.

16 figs, about 2¼ pounds
4 cups superfine sugar,
    plus more to coat
1 tablespoon cider vinegar

makes 16

On day 1: wash the figs and reserve. Put the sugar and vinegar in a large pan with 1¼ cups of water and bring slowly to a boil. Add the figs, turn down to a simmer and cook gently for 30 minutes. Remove from the heat and leave to cool in the liquid.

On day 2: bring the pan back to a simmer and cook for 1 hour. Leave to cool in the liquid as before.

On day 3: return the pan to a simmer and cook for a final 30 minutes. Leave to cool completely. Then, with a slotted spoon, remove the figs from the syrup and transfer to a wire rack. Put to dry for several hours in the sun if you can. When dry, toss individually in more sugar and store between layers of parchment paper in an airtight container.

sugar cookies

Machine production of puff pastry produces an excellent consistent flaky pastry, although most of it is made with vegetable oil. If you can find frozen puff pastry made with butter, then that is the one to buy.

scant 1 cup confectioner's sugar
½ pound puff pastry

makes 14

Preheat an oven to 475°F. Dust a work surface with some of the sugar and roll pastry out into a 10-inch square. Dust with more sugar. Fold both sides in to the middle, then fold one-half on top of the other. Cut into 1-inch-wide strips. Turn these on their side, cut side up, and dust with more sugar. Flatten with heel of hand, then roll into long shapes as thin as a sheet of pasta.

Transfer to a baking sheet and cook immediately for 5 to 6 minutes until a dark golden brown. With an icing spatula, remove to a wire rack and, when cool, dust with a little more icing sugar.

large ANZAC biscuits

These sweet biscuits, or cookies, named after the armed forces of Australia and New Zealand, were first made some 80 years ago. Successive generations have rediscovered them with the same delight.

scant ½ cup unsalted butter
1 tablespoon golden syrup
2 cups rolled oats
⅔ cup self-rising flour
⅔ cup superfine sugar
1 teaspoon baking soda

makes 12

Preheat an oven to 350°F.

In a pan, melt the butter with the golden syrup and 1 tablespoon of water. Remove from the heat and, when cool, beat in the remaining ingredients with a wooden spoon.

Roll the mixture into balls with a diameter of about 1½ inches. Put 4 on each of 3 baking sheets, pressing each down gently to flatten it. Bake for 30 minutes, when they will be golden brown.

Allow to cool completely on a rack before eating.

almond cookies

scant ½ cup unsalted butter,
 diced
1 cup superfine sugar
¾ cup slivered almonds
5 tablespoons orange juice
grated zest of 1 small orange

makes 20 to 25

Preheat an oven to 350°F. Put the butter into a mixing bowl and allow to soften at room temperature. When soft, add all the other ingredients and beat together with a wooden spoon until thoroughly combined.

Put heaped teaspoonfuls of this mixture on a nonstick baking sheet or on a baking sheet lined with parchment paper. They will spread as they bake, so make 4 or 5 rows of 5 biscuits, leaving plenty of space between them.

Bake for 15 to 20 minutes, until crisp and golden brown. Remove to a wire rack to allow to cool completely before serving.

crostoli

Crostoli are fried Italian pastries, although you may find them called other things, as there are many variations on the theme, depending on which part of Italy the people making them come from. It is very easy to make vanilla confectioners' sugar. Simply split a vanilla bean and put it in a clean dry jar and fill with sieved confectioners' sugar. Leave for weeks or even months. The flavor will continue to get stronger.

scant 1¼ cups self-rising flour,
 sifted
scant 1¼ cups all-purpose flour
3 tablespoons superfine sugar
1 teaspoon grated lemon zest
3 eggs
2 tablespoons sweet vermouth
3 tablespoons olive oil
sunflower oil, for deep-frying
confectioners' sugar (see above),
 to dust

makes 12 to 16

Sift the flours into a mixing bowl and add the sugar and lemon zest. Beat the eggs lightly and add them, together with the vermouth and olive oil. Form the mixture into a ball of dough. Flour a work surface and roll this out as thinly as pasta. Use a ravioli wheel to cut the sheet of dough into different shapes (doing a selection of all three or just one; it's up to you because they all cook and taste the same way). Using 2½-by-¾-inch strips: cut each down the center, leaving ½ inch uncut at one end. Plait the two lengths together. Using 2½-by-¾-inch rectangles: make two 2-inch parallel cuts lengthwise in the middle to allow pastry to open out during cooking. Using 2¾-by-¾-inch strips: tie each into a bow or knot.

Preheat the oil in a deep-fryer to 375°F. Fry the pastries in batches for 2 to 3 minutes each, until golden brown. Drain on paper towels, then dust with confectioners' sugar. Eat at once.

desserts

7

butternut squash tart

Butternut squash has a lovely orange color and, since the flesh is not strongly flavored, lends itself as readily to sweet treatments as it does to savoury.

1 recipe quantity sweet pastry
  (page 152)
2¼ cups diced (1-inch) peeled,
  seeded butternut squash
½ teaspoon salt
1 cup whole milk
scant ¾ cup superfine sugar
2 whole eggs, plus 1 yolk
7 tablespoons heavy cream
1 teaspoon ground cinnamon
½ teaspoon ground ginger
½ teaspoon ground nutmeg
¼ teaspoon ground cloves
heavy cream, to serve

serves 8

Preheat an oven to 350°F. Roll out the rested pastry and use it to line a 9½-inch tart pan that is 1 inch deep. Line with parchment paper, weight and bake blind for 10 minutes. Remove the weights and paper. Leave the oven on at the same temperature.

Put the squash in a pan and cover with water. Add the salt and bring to a boil. Cook for 10 minutes, drain in a colander and leave for 5 minutes to drain off excess moisture.

Put the pumpkin into a food processor and blitz to a fine purée, then add the milk, sugar, beaten eggs and extra yolk, the cream and spices. Continue to work until well amalgamated.

Pour into the tart shell and bake for 50 minutes. Allow to cool before cutting and serving with cream.

macadamia nut tart

The texture and sweetness of this pie is reminiscent of pecan pie.

1 recipe quantity sweet pastry
  (page 152)
1 cup unsalted macadamia nuts
½ cup light brown sugar
½ cup golden syrup
2 tablespoons unsalted butter
1 egg, beaten

Preheat an oven to 350°F. Roll out the pastry and use to line a 9½-inch tart pan that is 1 inch deep. Line with parchment paper, weight and bake blind for 10 minutes. Remove the weights and paper. Leave the oven on at the same temperature.

Put the macadamia nuts in a food processor and pulse-chop to a coarse texture. Melt the sugar in a saucepan with the golden syrup

½ cup soft white bread crumbs
confectioners' sugar, for dusting
lightly whipped cream, to serve

serves 8

and butter, being careful not to allow it to boil. Remove from the heat and leave to cool. Mix 1 tablespoon water and the beaten egg into this well, then add the crushed nuts followed by the bread crumbs. Pour the mixture into the tart shell.

Bake for 25 minutes, when the tart will have set and be a light golden brown. Remove and allow to cool slightly before dusting with a little confectioners' sugar. Serve with lightly whipped cream.

coconut tart

This makes the perfect light end to a warm summer lunch.

1 recipe quantity sweet pastry
   (page 152)
3 whole eggs, plus 2 yolks
½ cup superfine sugar
2¼ cups canned coconut milk
   (page 156)
1 piece peeled pumpkin,
   about 2 ounces
confectioners' sugar, for dusting
slices of ripe mango or
   pineapple, to serve

serves 8

Preheat an oven to 350°F. Roll out the pastry and use to line a 9½-inch tart pan that is 1 inch deep. Line with parchment paper, weight and bake blind for 10 minutes. Take out of the oven, remove the weights and paper and reserve. Turn down the oven to 300°F.

In a bowl, whisk the whole eggs, egg yolks and sugar together, then whisk in the coconut milk. Pass through a sieve into another bowl.

Cut the pumpkin into matchstick strips and blanch these in boiling water for 20 seconds. Refresh under cold running water. Drain in a sieve.

Pour the coconut custard into the tart shell and sprinkle the pumpkin sticks over the top. Bake for 1 hour 10 minutes, remove from the oven and allow to cool.

When cool, dust with confectioners' sugar before cutting into slices with a sharp knife, heating the blade first by dipping it in very hot water. Serve with slices of ripe mango or pineapple.

133

blueberry and syrup tart with cream

This is best made when blueberries are in season, although with the global larder they can of course be obtained all year round, if you are willing to pay a premium.

1 recipe quantity sweet pastry
  (page 152)
2½ tablespoons sugar
1½ cups blueberries
½ cup golden syrup
3 eggs
1¼ cups heavy cream
½ cup ground almonds
confectioners' sugar,
  for dusting
more heavy cream,
  to serve

serves 8

Preheat an oven to 350°F.

Roll out the pastry and use it to line a 9½-inch tart pan that is 1 inch deep. Leave to rest for 20 minutes.

Line the pastry shell with parchment paper, weight it, put the pan on a baking sheet and bake blind for 10 minutes. Remove from the oven, remove the weights and paper and put the shell to one side until needed.

Put the sugar in a pan with ⅔ cup of water. Bring to a boil, add the blueberries and blanch for 15 seconds. Strain through a colander or sieve and leave to drain for 10 minutes before using

Put the golden syrup into a small saucepan and warm over the lowest heat.

Break the eggs into a bowl. Add the cream and whisk together until smoothly amalgamated. Whisk in the ground almonds and the warm syrup. Distribute the blueberries evenly over the tart base and pour over the custard.

Put in the oven on the baking sheet and bake for 30 minutes, when the custard will be set. Remove and allow to cool slightly before dusting with confectioners' sugar.

Cut into wedges and serve with heavy cream.

quince and polenta crumble

2¼ pounds quinces (about 3
  large ones)
½ cup superfine sugar
juice of ½ lemon
1¾ cups heavy cream, to serve

for the crumble:
scant ¾ cup unsalted butter at
  room temperature, diced
1¼ cups polenta
scant 1¼ cups self-rising flour
¼ cup superfine sugar

serves 6

Put the sugar and lemon juice in a pan with 1¼ cups of water and bring to a boil. Turn down to a simmer. Peel, quarter and core the quinces, then cut the flesh into thick slices. Add to the syrup and cook for 45 minutes. Strain through a colander, reserving the syrup, and leave to cool.

Preheat an oven to 350°F.

Make the crumble: put the butter into a bowl and allow to soften at room temperature. When soft, rub in the other ingredients to a coarse crumb consistency, which takes about 4 minutes. It does not matter if you get some of it holding in larger lumps.

Spread the quince pieces to cover the bottom of a 10-inch-long, deep-sided baking dish to a depth of about 1½ inches. Top evenly with the crumble and bake for 1 hour.

About 5 minutes before it is due to come out of the oven, warm the syrup through and put into a pitcher for people to help themselves, also offering heavy cream at the table.

quince and amaretto tart with mascarpone

2¼ pounds quinces (about 3
  large ones)
scant ½ cup superfine sugar
juice of ½ lemon
1 recipe quantity sweet pastry
  (page 152)
scant ¼ cup slivered almonds
confectioners' sugar, for dusting
6 ounces mascarpone, about ¾
  cup, to serve

for the amaretto paste:
heaping ½ cup unsalted butter

Peel, quarter, slice and cook the quince as for quince and polenta crumble above, but leave the fruit in the syrup to cool.

Make the amaretto paste: remove the butter from the refrigerator ahead of time, cut it into dice and put it in a mixing bowl to soften. Cream it with the sugar until pale and fluffy.

Mix the ground almonds and flour together. In a small bowl, beat the eggs. Beat a spoonful of egg into the butter cream, followed by a tablespoonful of the almond mixture. Whisk continuously as you repeat these additions, only adding more when the last has been completely incorporated, until you have a light, creamy almond paste. Finally, whisk in the amaretto.

desserts

scant ½ cup superfine sugar
¾ cup ground almonds
1½ tablespoon all-purpose flour
2 eggs
2 tablespoons amaretto liqueur

serves 10

Preheat an oven to 350°F. Roll out the pastry and use it to line a 10-inch tart pan. Leave to rest for 20 minutes. Fill it with the briefly drained moist quince slices, then top with the almond cream. Smooth and level the surface with an icing spatula, then sprinkle the slivered almonds over the top.

Bake for 1 hour, remove from the oven and allow to cool.

When cool, dust with confectioners' sugar before slicing and serving with a generous spoonful of mascarpone on the side.

pavlova with a passion fruit curd

This is an ideal light summer dessert, which can be prepared a day or two ahead, leaving only the brief final assembly to be done before serving.

whites of 4 eggs
¾ cup superfine sugar
1 teaspoon white wine vinegar
1 tablespoon hot water
1¼ cups heavy cream

for the passion fruit curd:
2 whole eggs, plus 2 yolks
pulp from 4 fresh passion fruit
  with seeds (about 5
  tablespoons)
2 tablespoons unsalted butter,
  diced finely
¼ cup superfine sugar

serves 4

Preheat an oven to 300°F. Oil a large piece of parchment paper on a baking sheet.

Put the egg whites, sugar, vinegar and hot water in the bowl of a stand mixer and whisk at the highest speed for 5 minutes until you have soft white peaks of meringue. Spoon the mixture into an 8-inch round on the oiled paper. Cook in the center of the oven for about 1 hour 10 minutes, or until crisp. Allow to cool on a wire rack.

Make the passion fruit curd: put all the ingredients in a bowl set over a pan of simmering water and stir constantly until it starts to thicken and take on the appearance of a thin custard. Continue to cook and stir until this thickens further. As a rough guide this takes about 10 minutes from start to finish, but remove from the heat as soon as it thickens as you don't want to overcook it. Scrape the curd into a clean jar or container with a lid and leave to cool before refrigerating.

To assemble, whisk the cream into soft peaks and pour and scrape on to the pavlova base, spreading out to the edges with an icing spatula. Top with the passion fruit curd. Cut and serve at the table.

passion fruit caramel with sugar cookies

If fresh passion fruit is unavailable, the pulp sold in cans or cartons can be substituted.

3 whole eggs, plus 1 yolk
7 tablespoons whole milk
7 tablespoons heavy cream
7 passion fruits, to yield ½ cup
  pulp
heaping ½ cup superfine sugar
4 or 8 sugar cookies
  (page 128)

serves 4

Put half of the sugar and 3 tablespoons of cold water in a small pan and bring to a boil over medium heat, cooking until the syrup starts to color. At this point, turn the heat to low and allow the syrup to become a dark golden brown. Add another 2 tablespoons of water and stand back as the caramel surges and bubbles furiously before subsiding. Pour equal amounts immediately into each of 4 small molds.

Preheat an oven to 300°F. Put a roasting pan filled with 1¼ to 1½ inches of water over the heat and bring to a simmer.

Whisk the whole eggs and yolk in a bowl, then whisk in the milk and cream. Pass through a sieve into a second bowl. Add the passion fruit pulp and remaining sugar and whisk in. Pour into the molds.

Sit the molds in the water bath and put it into the oven. Bake for 50 to 55 minutes, when the custards will be set. Remove and leave to cool in the water, before refrigerating for at least 2 hours or overnight.

Turn out and serve with 1 or 2 sugar cookies per plate.

blood orange syrup cake

This cake has a wonderfully moist texture and a distinct citrus flavour from the whole blood oranges used in the cooking.

3 blood oranges
6 tablespoons unsalted butter,
  plus more for greasing
¾ cup superfine sugar
3 medium eggs
1¼ cups semolina flour
scant 1 cup self-rising flour
1 teaspoon baking powder
¾ cup milk
1¼ cups crème fraîche, to serve
for the orange syrup:
heaping ¾ cup superfine sugar
1½ cups blood orange juice

for the candied orange:
heaping 1 cup superfine sugar
1 blood orange, unpeeled and cut
  into thin slices

serves 10

Preheat an oven to 350°F and line an 8-inch springform cake pan with parchment paper and grease with butter.

Put one of the oranges in a saucepan, cover with water and bring to a boil. Turn down the heat and simmer for 1½ hours, topping up the water to cover as necessary. Leave to cool, then remove from the liquid and cut in half. Remove and discard any seeds, then put into a food processor or blender. Juice the remaining oranges and put the juice with the halved orange and blitz to a purée. Measure ⅔ cup and reserve.

Melt the butter in a saucepan. Put the sugar in a mixing bowl, pour over the butter and then whisk in the eggs, followed by the reserved orange purée, the semolina flour, self-rising flour and baking powder. Beat in well, then stir in the milk.

Pour the mixture into the cake pan and bake for 50 to 60 minutes, until set and golden brown. Remove and leave to cool in the pan.

Make the syrup by putting the superfine sugar and ¾ cup of the orange juice in a pan. Bring to a boil and boil for 2 minutes. Add the remaining juice and remove from the heat. Slowly pour the syrup over the cake, allowing it to soak in. Repeat until all the syrup is used up, then leave to cool.

Make the candied orange: in a pan dissolve the sugar in 1½ cups water and bring to a boil. Add the orange slices, lower the heat and simmer for 15 minutes. Remove from the heat and leave to cool.

Remove the cake from its pan and peel away the parchment paper. Cut into wedges and serve on large plates with several slices of the candied orange and a large spoonful of crème fraîche.

dark chocolate fudge cake

14 ounces dark chocolate
12 eggs
scant ¾ cup superfine sugar
1½ cups unsalted butter,
  softened
1¼ cups all-purpose flour
for the icing:
½ cup heavy cream
8½ ounces dark chocolate

serves 10

Preheat an oven to 300°F. Line a 9½-inch springform cake pan with parchment paper and butter it.

Melt the chocolate for the cake in a bowl set over a pan of simmering water. Put the eggs, sugar, butter and flour in a mixing bowl and whisk for 10 minutes until light and fluffy. Add the melted chocolate and whisk for 10 more minutes, then pour into the prepared pan.

Bake for 20 to 25 minutes. Remove and leave to cool. Take the cake from the pan, remove the parchment paper and place on a wire rack.

Make the icing: bring cream to a boil in a small pan. While it is heating, chop chocolate into small pieces. Remove cream from heat as it come to a boil and stir in chocolate. As soon as it has melted, pour mixture over cake. Smooth over top and round sides with an icing spatula. Allow to set before cutting with a warm knife.

espresso chocolate tart

1 recipe quantity sweet pastry
  (page 152)
7 ounces dark chocolate, broken
  into pieces
heaping ½ cup unsalted butter,
  diced
2 tablespoons strong espresso
  coffee
¾ cup cocoa powder
2 whole eggs, plus 2 yolks
scant ¼ cup superfine sugar
confectioners' sugar, to dust
lightly whipped cream, to serve

serves 8

Preheat an oven to 400°F. Roll out the pastry and use to line a 9½-inch tart pan. Cover with parchment paper, weight and bake blind for 10 minutes. Remove from the oven and turn the setting down to 300°F. Remove the weights and paper.

In a bowl set over barely simmering water, melt the chocolate and the butter. When completely melted, whisk in the coffee and the cocoa.

At the same time, in an electric mixer fitted with a balloon whisk, whisk the eggs, extra yolks and sugar until pale and creamy.

Fold the warm chocolate mixture into this cream, mixing well, and pour into the tart shell. Bake for 15 minutes. Leave to cool.

Dust with confectioners' sugar, cut into 8 wedges with a hot knife and serve with lightly whipped cream.

rich chocolate and roasted almond torte

This rich, moist torte is particularly good to eat with a cup of strong espresso.

heaping ¾ cup unsalted butter,
   diced, plus more for greasing
6½ ounces dark chocolate,
   broken into pieces
6 eggs, separated
heaping ¾ cup superfine sugar
heaping 1 cup coarsely ground
   roasted almonds

for the icing:
7 tablespoons heavy cream
5½ ounces dark chocolate,
   broken into small pieces

serves 10

Preheat an oven to 375°F. Cut a piece of parchment paper to line a 10-inch springform cake pan. Grease with butter and reserve.

Melt the butter and chocolate together in a bowl over barely simmering water. While they are melting, cream the egg yolks and sugar in a stand mixer fitted with a balloon whisk until pale and light, which takes about 8 to 10 minutes. Continuing to whisk, add the melted chocolate and butter. Stop the machine, remove the whisk and fold in the almonds with a metal spoon.

In a clean glass or metal bowl, whisk the egg whites to stiff peaks. Throw a spoonful into the chocolate mixture and stir it in to lighten it before folding in the rest.

Pour the mixture into the prepared springform pan and bake for 20 minutes. Turn down the temperature to 325°F and continue cooking for a further 40 minutes.

Remove and allow to cool in the pan set on a rack and covered with a damp cloth until completely cold. Remove the thin crust which will have formed on top of the cake with an icing spatula and discard. Turn out of the pan and remove the paper.

Make the frosting by bringing the cream to a boil in a small pan. Add the chocolate and remove from the heat, rapidly beating the chocolate in with a wooden spoon as it melts. Ice the top and sides of the cake. Allow it to cool and set before cutting.

spiced loquats and ginger ice cream

Loquats are indigenous to China and Southeast Asia. Orange in color and shaped like an egg, their taste and smell are reminiscent of those of crab apple, although they are not nearly so tart. Avoid ones that are marked or bruised, and they should feel quite firm when gently squeezed. The dark, chestnut-colored seeds should be discarded after poaching the fruit.

14 ounces loquats (about 8)
½ cup superfine sugar
2 lemon slices
2 fresh ginger slices
2 cinnamon sticks
3 star anise
2 or 3 blades of mace

for the ginger ice cream:
4½ ounces fresh ginger
¾ cup superfine sugar
4 egg yolks
1¼ cups heavy cream

serves 4

The day before, make the ice cream: grate the ginger on the finest plate of a grater or cut into pieces and blitz to a purée with 1 tablespoon of water. Put the mulch in cheesecloth and squeeze to extract the juice into a small bowl and reserve.

In a small heavy-bottomed saucepan, dissolve the sugar in 1 cup water. Bring to a boil over high heat, then leave to cook until it reaches 285°F on a candy thermometer, about 10 minutes.

At the same time, whisk the egg yolks in an electric mixer until pale, which takes about 4 minutes.

When the sugar syrup is ready, add the ginger juice and return to a boil. Remove from the heat, switch the mixer back on and pour the syrup over the egg yolks in a thin stream. Continue whisking until the mixture has tripled in volume. By this time it will have cooled. Turn off the mixer. Whip the cream to soft peaks and fold it in. Pour into a plastic container, cover with the lid and freeze overnight.

The next day, poach the loquats: in a heavy-bottomed saucepan, dissolve the sugar in 2 cups water and add the remaining flavoring ingredients. Over high heat, bring to a boil, then turn down to a simmer. Peel the loquats by stripping off the skin from top to bottom. Add to the syrup and simmer for 5 to 10 minutes. Turn off the heat and leave the loquats in the syrup until cool. When cool, cut the loquat in half and remove the seeds.

To serve, divide the loquats among 4 bowls, spoon over some of the strained syrup and a add large scoop of the ice cream.

lemon granita

Granita is the ubiquitous crunchy ice of the Mediterranean, as popular today in Greece as in Italy, the country that gave its name. The majority of Greek and Italian immigrants to Australia landed in Fremantle and their influence soon permeated the port with a wave of corner grocery shops and cafés, always the first to open and the last to close. In the height of the fierce Western Australian summer, cool granitas flavored with lemon, lime, melon, orange and coffee were to be had in every café. Under a burning sun there is nothing quite like a granita, served in a tall frosted glass with a long spoon and a straw to drink the sweet liquid as the heat melts the ice.

scant 1 cup lemon juice
½ cup superfine sugar

makes 4

The day before: put the lemon juice and sugar in a pan with 2 cups water and bring to a boil, stirring occasionally, until sugar is completely dissolved. Let cool to room temperature, then pour it into a shallow tray that will fit in the freezer.

Freeze for about 1 hour, until ice crystals start to form. Remove and stir with a fork, then return to the freezer for a second hour. Remove and again stir with a fork, scraping away from the sides and base where it freezes first and dragging from side to side. Return to the freezer for a third hour, then stir for a final time and freeze overnight.

About 10 minutes before serving, put 4 tall glasses in the freezer to chill. When frosted, remove and fill with the granita. Put the glasses on small plates, with a long spoon and a straw on each.

melon granita

In Australia rock melon would provide the ideal flesh for this granita, although any heavily perfumed melon — such as a Charentais or Persian — is fine.

1 very ripe melon, about 3½
   pounds
juice of ¼ lemon
¼ cup superfine sugar

serves 4

Cut the melon in half and scoop out the seeds into a sieve over a bowl to catch all the sweet liquid. Cut the halves into quarters and cut out the flesh, going close to the skin but being careful not to take off any of the outer strip next to the skin. Cut the flesh into pieces and put in a food processor with the collected juice, the lemon juice and sugar. Reduce to a purée, then prepare as for lemon granita above.

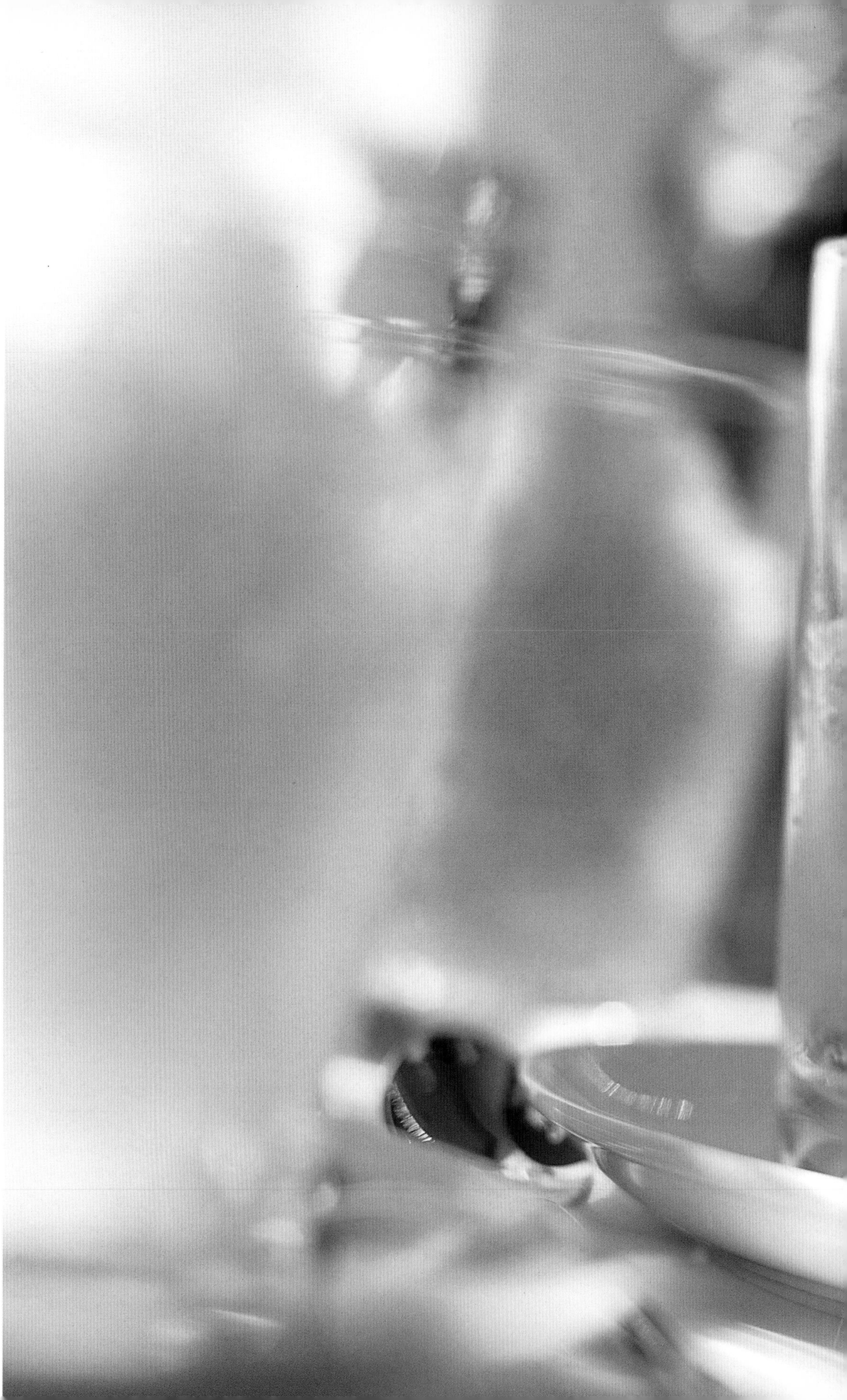

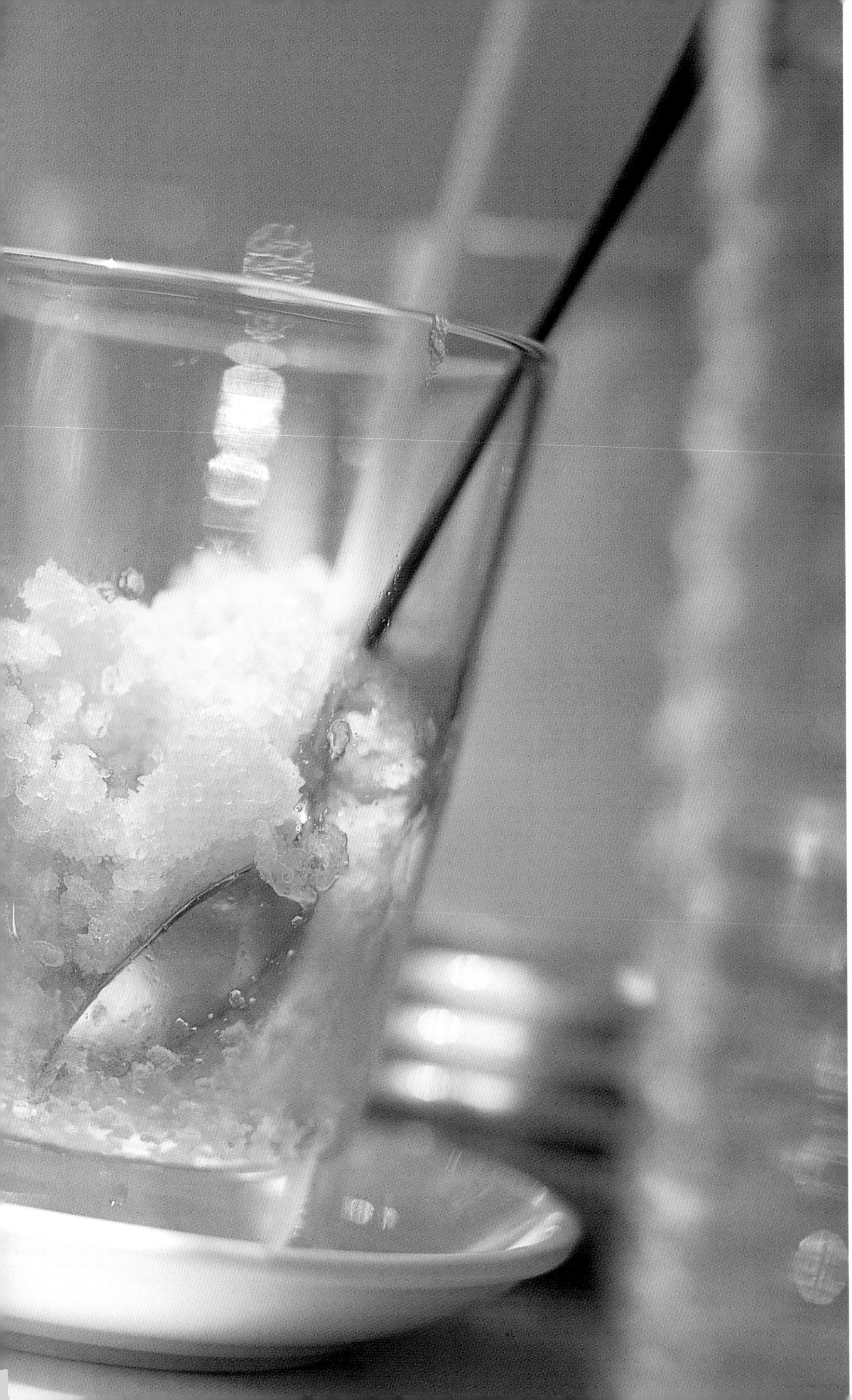

kulfi ice cream with poached guavas

Seasonally available, fresh guavas are sold by West Indian and Asian grocers. Select firm unbruised fruit. Kewra water can be bought from Indian shops.

15 cardamom pods
¼ cup ground almonds
2¼ cups whole milk
heaping ⅓ cup superfine sugar
2 or 3 drops kewra essence
 (optional; page 156)
¼ cup crushed unsalted
 pistachio nuts
4 egg yolks
1¼ cups heavy cream

for the poached guavas:
4 guavas
½ cup superfine sugar
1 teaspoon lemon juice

serves 4

Make the kulfi the day before: in a heavy-bottomed saucepan, put the milk and cardamom pods over medium heat and slowly bring to a boil. Turn down to a gentle simmer and reduce for 30 minutes, stirring from time to time.

When you have about ⅔ cup, add the sugar and almonds. Simmer for 2 more minutes, then strain through a fine sieve. If using kewra essence, add it now.

In an electric mixer, whisk the egg yolks until pale, then add the reduced milk mixture in a thin stream. Continue whisking for 5 to 6 minutes longer, when the mixture will have cooled and doubled in volume.

Lightly whip the cream to soft peaks. Add the pistachios and, using a large metal spoon, fold in together. Make sure everything is well combined before pouring into a plastic container with a lid and freezing overnight.

To poach the guavas: put 1¼ cups water in a pan with the sugar and lemon juice and bring to a boil. Lower the heat to a medium simmer. Cut the guavas into 3 or 4 thick rings and add to the syrup, then cook gently for 4 or 5 minutes. Remove from the heat and leave to cool in the syrup.

To serve: scoop 2 or 3 large spoonfuls of kulfi into each of bowls, add several slices of guava and spoon over the syrup.

black rice pudding with pandan leaf and coconut

Treated here as a pudding, this dish is more usually sold cold as a breakfast food in Malaysia and Indonesia. Pandan leaves (see page 157) impart an aromatic flavor to sweet and savory foods. Although available frozen, the whole point is their freshness and they can be bought from Southeast Asian shops, as can the glutinous black rice.

1½ cups black glutinous rice
3 fresh pandan leaves
heaping 1⅓ cups palm sugar
1¼ cups canned coconut milk
  (page 156), to serve

serves 4

Put the rice in a heavy-bottomed or nonstick pan with 9 cups of water and bring to a boil. Skim and lower the heat to a bare simmer. Add the pandan leaves and stir in, then cook for 1½ hours, stirring at regular intervals. The rice will be soft and have imparted a dark purple color to the now thickened cooking liquid.

Add the sugar and simmer for 10 minutes. Discard the leaves before serving with the coconut milk spooned over the top.

preserves & basic recipes

green tomato pickle

This is a good pickle to eat with cheese or cold meats. It needs at least a month to mature to its full flavor.

2 pounds green tomatoes
1⅛ pounds white onions
heaping ½ cup salt
1¾ cups distilled white vinegar
1½ cups superfine sugar
½ teaspoon allspice
½ teaspoon curry powder
½ tablespoon dry English mustard
½ tablespoon ground turmeric
4½ tablespoons all-purpose flour
makes about 4 pounds

Wash and cut out the cores of the tomatoes, then cut each into 5 or 6 pieces. If very large, cut them into large dice. Put into a large bowl. Chop the onions into pieces the same size and add.

Make a brine by boiling the salt with 2¼ cups water. Pour this over the tomatoes and onions and leave to stand overnight.

Drain through a colander, put into a pan with the vinegar, sugar and allspice and bring to a boil.

In a bowl, put the curry powder, mustard, turmeric and flour and whisk in 7 tablespoons water to make a smooth paste. Add to the gently boiling pickle mixture and stir in. It will have an immediate thickening effect. Continue to simmer for 5 minutes, stirring from time to time.

Leave to cool slightly before packing into sterilized jars. Store for at least a month before eating, longer if possible as the flavor continues to develop.

lemon pickle

The recipe for this pickle came from an Indian lady in the desert village of Pushka in Rajasthan, northern India, where it was served as part of a *thali* (a tray of small dishes) that included fresh curd, chapati, sweet tomato curry, mustard greens and boiled rice.

Properly, the pickle should be allowed to mature for a total of 4 or 5 months. If the climate or season do not make this possible, however, an excellent result can be achieved in the airing cupboard or on top of a hot water boiler, where it will eventually turn from a bright yellow to a burnt umber, its flavor by this time remarkable.

Jaggery is Indian raw lump sugar. Look for some which crumbles easily and is not hard as rock. If unobtainable, use palm sugar and, failing that, soft brown sugar.

1¾ pounds lemons, well scrubbed
½ cup salt
2¼ pounds jaggery or 6 cups soft brown sugar
about ½ tablespoon red pepper flakes
makes about 4 pounds

Halve and juice the lemons, reserving the juice. Cut the skins into ½-inch-wide strips. Put these in a large sterilized glass jar and pour over the lemon juice to cover by a depth of ½ inch. If there is not enough juice, squeeze some more, as this depth is important. Add the salt, screw the lid on tightly and turn the jar several times to distribute it evenly.

Put the jar in a sunny place or somewhere very warm and leave for 1 month.

At the end of that time, open the jar and add the sugar and pepper flakes, put the lid back on and turn to distribute evenly. Put back in the same place and leave for a further month, turning from time to time.

The pickle is now ready to eat, though it is a good idea at this point to taste and adjust the balance by adding more salt, sugar or pepper flakes as your taste dictates. Put the jar in a cool, dark place and leave undisturbed for at least 3 months and even longer before eating.

tamarind chutney

This chutney is good with any rice dish and its sweet-and-sour flavor works well with chicken or lamb.

7 ounce block tamarind (page 157)
2 tablespoons sunflower oil
1 teaspoon ground aniseeds
1 teaspoon red pepper flakes
2 tablespoons chopped fresh mint
½ cup soft dark brown sugar
salt
makes about 12 ounces

Break up the tamarind block and soak the pieces in warm water for 2 to 3 hours. Strain through a sieve, discarding the seeds and tough fibers but reserving the paste.

Heat the oil in a saucepan over medium heat. When hot, add the aniseeds. As soon as it gives off its characteristic aroma, add the pepper flakes, then 5 seconds later the tamarind paste, followed by the mint and ½ teaspoon salt.

Pour in 1½ cups water and stir in the sugar. Bring to a boil, lower the heat and simmer for 40 to 45 minutes, stirring from time to time.

Remove from the heat and leave to cool, before putting in a sterilized screw-top jar. Keep refrigerated.

japanese-style pickled ginger

½ cup Japanese rice vinegar
scant ¼ cup superfine sugar
¼ cup table salt
1 small slice beet
5½ ounces fresh ginger, peeled and cut into paper-thin slices
makes about 4 ounces

Bring the rice vinegar and sugar to a boil in a small saucepan. Remove and leave to cool.

In a second saucepan, bring 1¾ cups water to a boil with the table salt. Blanch the ginger in this for 2 minutes, drain and leave to cool.

Put ginger and beet in a sterile jar, secure with a tight-fitting lid and refrigerate for a week before using.

pasta dough

This basic pasta dough can be used for a variety of fresh noodles and filled pasta shapes, including lasagne, ravioli, agnolotti, pappardelle, fettuccine and tagliatelle. It can be held in the refrigerator or frozen and cooked straight from the freezer.

When rolling out pasta dough, the use of semolina flour is important. Ordinary flour tends to absorb moisture from the dough when you roll, whereas semolina flour prevents it from sticking and clogging. If you don't have any semolina, then ground polenta meal works well.

4⅔ cups all-purpose flour
5 eggs
4 tablespoons olive oil
semolina flour, for rolling
makes about 1½ pounds

Put the flour, eggs and olive oil in a food processor and pulse for 5 to 10 seconds until crumbly.

Transfer to a work surface and divide into quarters, gently pushing each into a compact ball. Wrap individually in plastic wrap and refrigerate for a minimum of 1 hour, and up to 3 hours.

Dust a work surface with semolina and put one ball of dough on top. Flatten slightly with the heel of your hand and dust with more flour before rolling out with a rolling pin until you achieve a thickness that will pass through the thickest setting on the pasta machine.

As you pass the rolled dough through the machine, continuously dust with semolina flour. Work successively through finer settings until you achieve the desired thickness — usually No. 1 or No. 2 setting.

Cut the — now long — sheets of pasta into 12-inch lengths, layer between sheets of parchment paper dusted with semolina flour and refrigerate until needed or freeze.

squid ink pasta

If not using this immediately, it can be frozen and cooked straight from the freezer.

4½ cups all-purpose flour
4 eggs
2½ tablespoons olive oil
4 packets of squid ink, 1 ounce
¼ teaspoon salt
makes about 1½ pounds

Put all the ingredients in a food processor and proceed as for the basic pasta dough on the previous page. Cut into fine strips, with the machine set for linguine.

sweet pastry

⅔ cup all-purpose flour
⅔ cup self-rising flour
¼ cup confectioners' sugar
heaping ½ cup chilled unsalted butter
1 egg
makes 2 round tart shells 9½ inches across and 1 inch deep

Cut the butter straight from the refrigerator into small dice and leave on a plate to soften.

Sift the flours and sugar into a mixing bowl and rub the butter in with your fingers to achieve a crumb consistency. Whisk the egg and add, working in gently to form a ball of dough. Divide in 2 and wrap in plastic wrap, then refrigerate for at least 30 minutes. Because of the high fat content, this resting phase is vitally important or you will have problems when rolling out.

After removing from the refrigerator, leave at room temperature for 5 minutes before rolling. This pastry may be frozen in balls or rolled out in tart pans. If the former, thawing is necessary before use, but a frozen tart shell can be baked blind straight from the freezer.

chicken stock

The ginger is only included for Asian dishes.

3 chicken carcasses
2 onions, coarsely chopped
2 carrots, coarsely chopped
2-inch piece fresh ginger, peeled and sliced (optional)
leaves from a head of celery, chopped
1 teaspoon peppercorns
makes about 1½ quarts

Put the chicken carcasses in a large saucepan and pour over 3½ quarts of cold water.

Bring to a boil, skim, lower the heat to a simmer and add the onions, carrots, the ginger, if using it, the celery leaves and the peppercorns. Simmer for 3 hours, skimming the surface from time to time.

Ladle the clear stock through a fine sieve into a clean saucepan and discard the solids. Boil to reduce by half for a strong chicken stock.

beef stock

The inclusion of a piece of calf's foot or pig's trotter both improves flavor and, by imparting natural gelatine, jellies the stock. On reduction, this effect is intensified, thickening sauces without the need for flour or any other agent.

2¼ pounds beef chuck bones
½ calf's foot or 1 pig's foot
1 large yellow onion, coarsely chopped
1 carrot, coarsely chopped
2 celery stalks, coarsely chopped
½ leek, coarsely chopped
2 or 3 fresh parsley sprigs
2 or 3 fresh thyme sprigs
2 bay leaves
½ teaspoon peppercorns
makes about 7½ cups

Preheat an oven to 475°F.

Put the beef bones and foot in a roasting pan and roast for about 1 hour, when they will be colored dark brown and most of the fat will have rendered.

Check at regular intervals that they are not burning, for if blackened, they will impart a bitter flavor.

Remove the bones and foot from the oven and put into a large pot. Cover with about 4 quarts cold water. Bring to a boil and skim thoroughly, then add the vegetables and aromatics. Lower the heat and simmer gently for 6 to 7 hours.

Remove the bones and vegetables with a slotted spoon, then pass the stock through a fine sieve. Allow to cool completely before refrigerating.

shrimp stock

3 garlic cloves
½ fennel bulb
I carrot
I celery stalk
I small yellow onion
3 fresh parsley sprigs
2 fresh tarragon sprigs
2 tablespoons olive oil
¼ pound shrimp shells
¼ teaspoon peppercorns
makes about 1½ quarts

Chop the vegetables into small pieces, but leave the herbs whole.

Put a saucepan over medium heat. Add the olive oil, followed by the shrimp shells. Cook for 2 minutes, then add the garlic and fennel. Cook for 2 to 3 minutes. Add the remaining ingredients and cook for a further 5 minutes, stirring from time to time.

Pour over 9 cups of cold water. Bring to a boil, skim, lower the heat and simmer gently for I hour.

Remove from the heat and pass through a fine strainer. Leave to cool completely before storing in the refrigerator.

vegetable stock

2 yellow onions
I or 2 carrots
2 celery stalks
4½ ounces fennel
2 garlic cloves
I tablespoon olive oil

2 fresh parsley sprigs
2 fresh thyme sprigs
2 bay leaves
½ teaspoon peppercorns
makes about 3¾ cups

Chop the vegetables into large pieces. In a large saucepan over medium heat, cook the vegetables in the olive oil for 2 to 3 minutes. Add the parsley, thyme, bay leaves and peppercorns.

Pour over 9 cups of cold water and bring to a boil. Lower the heat and simmer for I hour, skimming the surface frequently.

Pass through a fine strainer and allow to cool completely before refrigerating.

tomato vinaigrette

Serve this with any pasta, homemade gnocchi, fresh clams or mussels and grilled or roast fish.

1⅛ pounds ripe plum (Roma) or other
   vine-ripened tomatoes
⅔ cup olive oil
2 garlic cloves, finely chopped
2 shallots, finely chopped
2 tablespoons white wine vinegar
1¼ cups thin tomato purée
   (see tomato sauce, page 154)
I tablespoon chopped fresh basil leaves
I tablespoon chopped fresh tarragon leaves
I teaspoon balsamic vinegar
salt and pepper
makes about 2 cups

Blanch the tomatoes, cut them into quarters and seed.

In a saucepan over medium heat, warm 3 tablespoons of the oil and cook the garlic and shallots for 2 to 3 minutes. Add the white wine vinegar and reduce until syrupy. Add the tomato pieces, tomato purée, the herbs and the remaining oil. Lower the heat and simmer gently for I hour.

Remove from the heat and stir in the balsamic vinegar. Season with I teaspoon salt and ½ teaspoon pepper and leave to cool before passing through a sieve or a food mill.

Pour into a sterilized jar, cover tightly and store in the refrigerator until needed.

soft polenta

Once exclusively the food of the poor in northern Italy, polenta today enjoys an honored place on smart tables. Soft polenta made from proper old-fashioned polenta flour takes lengthy cooking and close attention from the cook, but ultimately delivers a superior result to instant polenta. However, the latter is very useful when time is at a premium and it does produce consistently good results, particularly when the polenta is combined with other ingredients.

⅔ **cup milk**
⅔ **cup light cream or half-and-half**
1 garlic clove, chopped but left whole
salt and pepper
scant ½ cup polenta
serves 4

In a heavy-bottomed saucepan, bring a mixture of 1½ cups water, the milk and two-thirds of the cream to a boil.

Add the garlic, 1 teaspoon of salt and 1 teaspoon of pepper. Turn down the heat to a simmer and whisk in the polenta until you have a porridgelike consistency.

Cook over low heat for 40 to 50 minutes, beating with a wooden spoon every 5 minutes and paying particular attention to the edges of the pan where there is the greatest tendency for the polenta to stick.

Beat in the remaining cream, cook for a final 2 minutes and remove from the heat. Pour and scrape into a warmed deep bowl and serve as an alternative to mashed potatoes, for example with the braised duck on page 77.

steamed jasmine rice

2½ cups Thai jasmine rice
serves 4 to 6

Put the rice in a saucepan that has a tight-fitting lid. Add a little cold water, swirl to wash and pour off.

Add 3½ cups of cold water and bring to a boil. Immediately turn down the heat to its lowest setting. Put on the lid and cook for precisely 15 minutes. Do not lift the lid!

After 15 minutes, turn off the heat and leave undisturbed for 10 minutes to allow the rice to steam dry, absorbing all of the water to give a perfect result. Only now should you remove the lid and serve.

tomato sauce

The Italian communities in Australia have a long established practice of making large quantities of sauce with each year's tomato crop, gathering as extended families and turning the occasion into a party after the long, hard day's work is done. The *pomodoro* — or passata — of cooked, sieved vine-ripened plum tomatoes flavored with basil, garlic and onion, is invariably stored in sterilized beer bottles and used throughout the year. Scrupulous hygiene is vital to prevent spoiling.

The sauce can either be left chunky or passed through a food mill to produce a uniform thin purée. The former is ideal for adding to stews, soups or meat sauces. The thinner sauce is better suited to dress spaghetti, ravioli or gnocchi. It is also good with barbecued meat and fish.

This amount will fill a 3½-cup jar or, when sieved, a beer bottle with the same capacity. Multiply the ingredients in the same proportions when making the most of a tomato glut.

3½ **pounds ripe plum (Roma) tomatoes**
⅔ **cup olive oil**
6 garlic cloves, finely chopped
1 yellow onion, finely chopped
3 or 4 fresh basil sprigs
salt and pepper
½ **teaspoon superfine sugar**
makes 3½ cups

Cut out and discard the cores of the tomatoes and cut them in 2, then squeeze out the seeds and pulp. Chop the flesh coarsely.

Put a large saucepan over medium-low heat. Add the oil and allow to warm through, then add the garlic, onion and chopped basil stems, gently sweating for a few minutes until soft. Add the chopped tomatoes and turn down the heat further, to cook slowly, stirring from time to time. When the tomatoes start to break down, add ½ teaspoon of salt, the sugar and the whole basil leaves. Grind in some pepper and continue to simmer for a total cooking time of 75 minutes, stirring from time to time.

While the sauce is cooking, sterilize the jar(s) or

bottle(s) in boiling water. (Bacteria, airborne natural yeasts and fungi are always lying in wait to help prepare your jams, chutneys and pickles for a premature demise.) Wash them first in hot water with detergent, then rinse them thoroughly. Put them in a large pan and cover completely with water. Bring to a boil and boil for 5 minutes. Remove with tongs and leave to steam dry. Lids and rubber sealing rings should be boiled, too. After filling, ideally store in a cupboard at an ambient temperature of 40° to 60°F.

When the sauce is ready, it can be left as it is or put through a food mill to produce a much thinner but uniform sauce. If you do the latter, you must reboil the sauce before pouring it through a sterilized funnel into the bottle.

Place the lid or cap on tightly. Put a rack in a large saucepan, stand the container on it and fill with hot water up to the neck. Bring to a simmer at 190°F and maintain this temperature for 30 minutes. Remove and leave to cool before storing.

toasted sesame seed mayonnaise

This goes particularly well with cold roast or barbecued chicken, or in a baguette or chicken salad sandwich.

1 teaspoon sesame seeds
1 garlic clove
salt and pepper
2 egg yolks
1½ teaspoon Dijon mustard
1 teaspoon white wine vinegar
1 cup sunflower oil
5 tablespoons Asian sesame oil
makes about 1¼ cups

In a small, dry frying pan over low heat, toast the sesame seeds, constantly stirring them until they color a light golden brown. Transfer to a bowl and reserve.

Put the garlic on a chopping board with slightly less than ¼ teaspoon of salt and grind the two together to a paste.

Put the egg yolks, mustard, vinegar and garlic paste in a mixing bowl and whisk to mix. Add the sunflower oil, starting by incorporating a few drops and, only

when it begins to hold, adding the oil in a thin stream.

Whisk in 1 tablespoon hot water, then slowly incorporate the sesame oil. Taste, adding pepper and more salt as you see fit. Finally, stir in the sesame seeds.

red curry paste

If feeling in a traditional mood, pound the ingredients by hand in a pestle and mortar. If a more techno-contemporary persuasion holds sway, use a food processor.

10 dried red chilies
1 teaspoon coriander seeds
1 teaspoon cumin seeds
4 large fresh red chilies, seeded
1-inch piece of fresh galangal, peeled and coarsely chopped
2 lemongrass stalks, topped and tailed, coarse outer leaves removed and coarsely chopped
2 tablespoons coarsely chopped fresh cilantro roots
1 kaffir lime leaf
3 red shallots, coarsely chopped
3 garlic cloves, coarsely chopped
1 teaspoon shrimp paste
3 tablespoons sunflower oil
salt and pepper
makes about ½ cup

Soak the dried chilies in tepid water for 10 minutes. Dry roast the coriander and cumin seeds in a frying pan over medium heat for 1 to 2 minutes, removing them when they start to color.

Put the toasted cumin and coriander seeds in a mortar with ½ teaspoon peppercorns and pound to a powder with a pestle, or simply grind to a powder in a coffee grinder. Put in a large bowl.

Drain the dried chilies and put them with the fresh chilies, galangal, lemongrass, cilantro roots, lime leaf, shallots and garlic in the mortar. Pound to a fine paste, adding the shrimp paste and 1 teaspoon salt at the end. Alternatively, work to a purée in a food processor.

Scrape the purée into the bowl with the spices, add the oil and mix well. This red curry paste can be stored in a screw-top jar in the refrigerator for several weeks.

glossary

Asafetida, or asafoetida, is a yellowish-brown hardened resin from India that has a peculiar smell in the can, but which imparts an intriguing flavor. It is the pungent extract of a root, and can be bought either in lump form or as a powder — the former is preferable. Asafoetida keeps for a long time in the can or jar, without losing its strong flavor. It is only ever used in small amounts. If using lumps, powder them in a coffee grinder or smash them with the flat of a heavy knife.

Basil is used extensively in Australia, both the European form and holy basil, also called Thai basil. This latter is a very different herb, with narrower leaves and a unique flavor akin to aniseeds. The two are not interchangeable.

Bean curd, or tofu, is a high-protein, soft and edible material made from soy milk, with a texture like that of a solid custard. It has almost no taste, picking up flavor from the dominant seasonings and aromatics with which it is cooked.

Belacan, balachan or blacan — shrimp paste — is an important Southeast Asian ingredient that can be bought in paste form or dried and compressed in cakes from Asian shops. It is made from partially decomposed salted shrimp and has an alarmingly pungent odor, particularly the paste variety which, when you first open the jar, can make even the most adventurous cook reel back ashen-faced. Don't worry: this pungency vanishes during cooking. The dried version is stronger flavored than paste. If you have difficulty finding the paste, use roughly half the amount of dried. Belacan is usually dry-roasted before use. The easiest way of doing this is to wrap the amount you need in foil and put it in an oven preheated to 350°F for 6 to 8 minutes. Let it cool before unwrapping and using. Keep the unused paste wrapped and in a screw-top jar in the refrigerator. Its applications are many and varied, from sambals to fried rice.

Black beans come from China, in cans and jars or dried, and are heavily salted, demanding a thorough rinse before use. Even then, care should be taken when seasoning. They are usually used to give both texture and flavor when finishing a sauce.

Bok choy is an Asian dark-leafed brassica, with crisp white stems, that is used extensively in Southeast Asian cooking. It should be lightly cooked.

Bulgur, also called burghul or bulghur, is a form of cracked wheat. It can be eaten as it is in salads or cooked.

Chilies exist in so many varieties that one could write an entire book about nothing else. The chili is now so ubiquitous in Southeast Asian cooking that it is odd to think that they originated in South America. A close relative of the sweet pepper, the chili is used fresh like an aromatic vegetable as one would onion and garlic, and when dried is used as a spice.

You can't tell how hot chilies are just by looking at them. All have slightly different flavors and heat intensity but, as a rough indicator, the smaller they are the more vicious — the tiny Thai green chili a case in point. The round red Scotch bonnet from the West Indies and the habanero from Mexico are among the hottest. The heat of the chili is concentrated in the seeds and the connecting membrane that holds them. Removing both will make the chili less hot.

Chinese chives are larger than ordinary chives, with a pronounced garlic aftertaste.

Choy sum is a smaller variant of bok choy, with green stems, sometimes sold in yellow flower. All parts can be eaten.

Coconut is central to the cultures of Southeast Asian countries, where virtually every part of the coconut palm tree on which it grows is used. We are most familiar with coconut flesh in its dried form, but this is not common in the countries where palm trees grow in wild abundance, though a limited amount of desiccated coconut features in desserts and sweets.

Coconut milk is one of the most important elements in Asian cooking and is used extensively in both savory and sweet dishes. This is not the clear sweet liquid you find inside coconuts, but the extract of fresh, shredded coconut flesh achieved by soaking it in water and then squeezing it.

Although you can buy fresh coconuts in some Asian markets, the word "fresh" is not always accurate and to the unfamiliar there is no way of knowing how old and dried out they are. It is preferable in these circumstances to use canned coconut milk.

Curry leaves are sold fresh and dried in Asian grocers and deliver a lovely, aromatic flavor. The fresh leaves are infinitely superior to dried and may be frozen.

Dashi is the essential soup stock of the Japanese kitchen and is made from konbu, a kelp seaweed, and dried bonito, a game fish. Japanese restaurants make their own dashi, using bonito graters rather like mandolines set in polished wooden boxes. Dashi-no-moto, instant dashi soup stock, can be bought in packets from Asian markets. The granules resemble dried yeast and only need to be whisked with hot water to make a delicious well-flavored stock.

Daikon is a large, mild-flavored white radish that is also called mooli. It is omni-present as a garnish in Japanese cooking.

Dried shrimps are used in a similar way to belacan, after rehydration in warm water.

Fish cake from China and Vietnam is very different from the Western version. It is made from the pounded flesh of different kinds of fish and is sold ready-cooked in rolls from the refrigerator cases of Asian stores. All you do is cut it in slices and heat them through, usually in liquid dishes like soups.

Fish sauce, perhaps more than any other ingredient, delivers the flavor that positions and differentiates the cooking of Southeast Asia, where it replaces salt. It is used as a sauce at the table like soy, often poured into a small bowl with lime juice and chili for people to help themselves, but also in cooking. Exposure to heat moderates its intense and complex flavor to the point that its origins cannot be determined. There is only a subtle alteration to the overall flavor, so you notice the absence of the sauce almost more than its inclusion.

The most common fish sauces are *nam pla* from Thailand and *nuoc mam* from Vietnam. Both are made from small sea fish and squid that are layered in huge wooden tubs with sea salt then left to ferment for several months. The liquid that this produces is drawn off into ceramic pots and left in the sun to mature for several weeks before being bottled, the first of several extractions — with the first being the lightest and finest. The result is a rich and mellow sauce that smells rather alarming to the uninitiated, but the taste of which is difficult to describe and certainly very different from what the strong odor leads you to expect. It is salty, and has affinities with soy sauce, but has a delicious and subtle fragrance on the palate that is quite unique.

Galangal, also called galanga, galangale, or *laos*, is a member of the ginger family and looks very similar, though the roots tend to be larger. The flavor is distinctive, rather more earthy than ginger but in a subtle way. If unobtainable fresh, galangal can be bought dried both as a powder and in slices, though when you can't get fresh, it is probably better to substitute fresh ginger.

Ikan bilis, a Malay speciality, is made from very small fish similar to whitebait, which are dried and salted. Ikan bilis are fried until crisp and sprinkled over rice dishes as a savory garnish.

Jaggery or loaf sugar comes from India and is made from the sap of the nippah palm. It is similar to the palm sugars of Southeast Asia.

Kaffir lime leaves are leaves from the Asian lime. They are a vivid green and deliver a terrific flavor. They can be bought fresh, frozen or dried, the third an inferior option.

Kecap manis is a thick Indonesian soy sauce sweetened with palm sugar. A.B.C. is a good brand. This is different from kecap asin, also called black sauce, which is salty and not at all sweet.

Kewra water is an intensely flavored extract of the Indian kewra plant and is used in desserts in the same way as rose water.

Lebanese cucumbers are small cucumbers with rather knobby skins and a slightly bitter flavor.

Long beans, also known as snake beans or yard-long beans, as their name suggests, are very long but have a similar — if slightly stronger — flavor to French beans.

Macadamia nuts are round and about the size of large hazelnuts. They are produced on a large scale in Australia, notably in New South Wales. They have only recently become popular in overseas markets, where they are quite expensive. They have a similar texture to Brazils and candlenuts and are used mainly in sweet dishes.

Maltose is rather like glucose, very sticky but with little flavor. It is sold in small pots in Chinese stores and supermarkets and is used to glaze poultry. It has to be heated gently before it liquefies.

Mangoes and papayas are used both ripe and in their green unripened state in savory dishes and in chutneys and pickles, where their high pectin levels are very useful. When buying them ripe, they should be very sweet and not all fibrous; the skins should be unblemished. Both will ripen over a few days at room temperature, wrapped in papèr. When ripe, they smell sweet and perfumed.

Masoor dal is the Indian term for red lentils, hulled, pink split peas that turn yellow when cooked.

Noodles are used in many different forms. Dry rice vermicelli are thin, almost translucent, noodles that can be used directly from the packet to fry crisp, otherwise they need a preliminary soaking, or are boiled briefly. Bought fresh, egg noodles — *lo mein* in Chinese and *ramen* in Japanese — may also be frozen and cooked straight from the freezer. They are yellow and sold in two thicknesses. Fresh rice noodles, also called rice sticks, are very thin and become transparent when cooked, usually in soups. *Soba* are Japanese buckwheat noodles, sold both fresh and (more commonly outside Japan) dried.

Nori is Japanese black green laver, a type of seaweed, and needs to be toasted before use. It is used for wrapping *sushi*, but can also be eaten grilled as a snack or crumbled over rice or noodles. Store in an airtight container.

Oils used in all dishes that are not European in origin are generally either sunflower or peanut because of their clarity and neutrality. Asian sesame oil, which is made from roasted sesame seeds and is both darker and more strongly aromatic than the cold-pressed version, is used more as a last-minute flavoring medium than a frying medium.

Olive oil is used extensively and we differentiate between different types only as olive oil, by which we mean good supermarket own-brand, and extra-virgin, which means very good, first-pressing oil of a low acidity from identified producers and a single geographic source. The latter does not automatically mean Italian, estate-bottled oils. Spain and Greece also produce exceptional olive oil. If you use a lot of olive oil it is a good idea to buy it in 2- or 4-quart cans, which offer substantial savings. Cans are also better for storage, as olive oil deteriorates more rapidly when exposed to light. Olive oil can be refrigerated, but its high fat content then causes it to solidify. This does it no harm and when brought back to room temperature it soon returns to its natural liquid state.

Palm sugar is made from the sap of the palmyra tree. This is simply boiled, producing a crystallized brown and sticky sugar that is sold in cans and as cellophane-wrapped cakes. It has a pronounced caramel flavor, but is not as sweet as cane sugar. It is sold in block form from Malaysia and Indonesia, while Thai palm sugar is sold as a thick syruplike treacle. While different from that of unrefined brown sugar, the flavor has obvious affinities with it and when unavailable, raw (demerara) sugar may be substituted.

Pancetta is traditionally cured Italian bacon and is sold in different grades and cuts. The finest is often thinly sliced and eaten raw like Parma ham. Good-quality bacon can therefore be substituted.

Pandan or pandanus leaves, also called screwpine leaves, are primarily used in sweet dishes. The leaves are bright green and resemble the palm leaves given to children on Easter Sunday. Pandan leaves are sold fresh and frozen and impart a lovely flavor, reminiscent of coconut.

Rice of several different types are used in this book. Thai rice, also called jasmine rice because of the aroma it gives off when cooked, is a superior white long-grain rice that is usually steamed. Glutinous rice — often called sticky rice — has a shorter, rounder grain and is often cooked with coconut milk. Black glutinous rice is, in reality, a purple brownish color and is common throughout Malaysia and Indonesia, where it is eaten in a rice pudding flavored with pandan leaves, coconut and palm sugar. Arborio, carnaroli and vialone nano are the three main types of risotto rice; any of them would be suitable for our recipes.

Rice vinegars from China and Japan are mild-flavored and available in both light, yellowish and darker-colored forms, like the much-admired Chinkiang brand black vinegar from Zheijang.

Rice wine is available in dry and sweet forms, the Japanese wines being *sake* and *mirin*. Shaoxing, Chinese rice wine, is used extensively in that country's cooking.

Salt in this book, unless otherwise described, always means sea salt.

Sambal oelek or red chili paste can be bought from supermarkets in jars or prepared fresh at home. In Malaysia it is sold freshly pounded in small plastic bags, and called "chili boh."

Shrimp paste, see belacan.

Sichuan pepper is a highly aromatic berry from northern China that needs to be dry roasted before grinding and is also used whole as an aromatic stock ingredient.

Soy sauce is made throughout Southeast Asia and is available in a bewildering variety, both dark and light and varying in thickness, saltiness and sweetness. These are qualities that can only be determined by tasting. The best Japanese soy sauce is Kikkoman, which is thin, dark and salty and is specified in all dishes with Japanese antecedents. Pearl River is an excellent dark full-flavored Chinese soy sauce. Use this or another Chinese product when the description "soy sauce" is given.

Soy milk is the thick, liquid soy by-product, made by soaking the dried beans, grinding them and then straining the results. It is used in drinks and desserts, particularly in countries that do not eat dairy products. It is now widely available.

Squid ink is now available in packets, the contents of which are very effective in dyeing risottos or pasta, but through processing have lost all their flavor, so always use in sauces in combination with a well-flavored fish or shellfish stock.

Star anise is an Asian spice used to imbue dishes with its powerful aniseed flavor.

Tamarind derives its name from the Arabic meaning "Indian dates," as it bears a passing visual resemblance to that fruit. It has a sour taste and is used extensively in Indian and Southeast Asian cooking. You find it in Asian grocers, peeled and seeded and wrapped in square packets. You should always bend and press a packet before buying to make sure it is pliant; if it has gone hard, it has dried out and you will not be able to extract much pulp. The pulp is then soaked in water and rubbed between the fingers. This extract is then strained through a sieve and it is this tamarind water that is used in cooking, the leftover solids being discarded. You can now also buy liquid tamarind extract, which is simply thinned with water in a ratio of about 10 to 1.

Tempeh is an Indonesian variation on the bean curd theme, and is also used in Malaysia and Singapore. It is rich in protein and vitamin B12, has no saturated fat and forms an edible mold on the surface. Like tofu it is sold fresh in slabs, but there is an unfortunate tendency to freeze it. Find out which day it is delivered and buy that day.

Thai celery, or *ceun chai*, is greener than ordinary celery, with a greater proportion of leaves to stalk and a much stronger flavor. When substituting ordinary celery, use the leaves but only the inner stalks.

Vietnamese mint resembles spearmint in appearance but not in taste. Its flavor is unique and is at the heart of a Penang *laksa*. It is only sold fresh and there is no substitute.

Wasabi is dried green powdered Japanese horseradish with a powerful flavor that can literally take your breath away and make your eyes water if eaten injudiciously. Traditionally an accompaniment to *sashimi* and *sushi*, it can also be used to boost the flavor of store-bought horseradish cream and to spike mayonnaise and other sauces.

157

index